GARLAND STUDIES IN

THE HISTORY OF AMERICAN LABOR

edited by

STUART BRUCHEY
UNIVERSITY OF MAINE

A GARLAND SERIES

NEW GAME, NEW RULES

Jobs, Corporate America, and the Information Age

ADELE GRAY
GINA ALPHONSO

GARLAND PUBLISHING, Inc.
New York & London / 1996

Library of Congress Cataloging-in-Publication Data

Gray, Adele.
New game, new rules : jobs, corporate America, and the
information age / Adele Gray and Gina Alphonso.
    p.   cm. — (Garland studies in the history of American
labor)
    Includes bibliographical references and index.
    ISBN 0-8153-2463-4 (alk. paper)
    1. Corporations—United States—History. 2. Business
enterprises—United States—History. 3. Entrepreneurship—United
States—History. 4. Information society—United States.
I. Alphonso, Gina. II. Title. III. Series.
HD2785.G73 1996
331.25—dc20
                              96-5264

Printed on acid-free, 250-year-life paper
Manufactured in the United States of America

Dedication

To our families, and friends, who have taught us there is more to life than work. To our companies, which have taught us about the rewards available in the marketplace. To our education, which gave us a time and place to pause and reflect on the marriage of work and family and friends.

Andi & Gina

My appreciation to Fred and Susan Isquith, who define the role of business and personal friendship through thick and thin. Thank you to Fred for helping me to see my way clear to practice at work the values I talk about in this book. My love and gratitude to Ed and Florence Cory Gray, who taught me to be an entrepreneur. All my love to Steve Goldenberg, a top notch feminist despite his macho demeanor, and to Robin Goldenberg, the next generation, and the one for whom this book was really written.

Andi

To Jean Mingo, the last generation, and Katie Alfonso, the next generation. My love to both.

Gina

Contents

Foreword

This book began as research for an independent study, as part of the Executive MBA program. The research began in 1992, and continues today. This research has changed the way we look at ourselves, our work and the companies in which we spend so much of our waking hours. We hope this book will generate a productive dialog about dealing with the changes at work that shape our entry into the 21st Century.

The work on this book was sponsored and supported by a wonderful gentleman and American business historian, Professor Stuart Bruchey, whose insight, guidance and patience have been invaluable. We first met Professor Bruchey when he taught a course in Conceptual Foundations—American Business history and perspective. We found his course, and his teaching, to be a valuable and necessary part of building a well rounded MBA. Through his course we better understood the history which frames who we are and what we do today in business, as well as that history's implications for tomorrow's workplace.

Our many thanks to a professor who is committed to the strength and wonder of the American Enterprise system. He taught us that leadership is based upon respect for the individual and upon ethical behavior. He taught us about the need to build flexible systems and processes in order to make money and contribute to society. We hope this book lives up to his expectations.

Andi Gray & Gina Alfonso
December, 1995

INTRODUCTION

This book is about changes nearly all of us face today at work, as our world shifts into the Information Age.

We began the work that resulted in this book because we personally were concerned about our careers, and about the companies in which we worked. We saw our friends and co-workers wrestling with similar concerns. We watched as our companies lost marketshare and good employees. We endured downsizings, rightsizings and leaves-without-pay. We saw fellow students, bright, talented, hard working individuals, pushed out of work for reasons that were not clear. We saw a growing loss of trust and commitment. Something was not working. We wanted to know why things were not working. We wanted to explore what could be done to change the workplace for the better.

We found that today's issues in the workforce and in companies point to critical problems that must be resolved. We believe that failure to address these critical problems will result in an underproductive workforce, uncompetitive companies, and a loss of leadership status in the global marketplace. We believe that these problems can be addressed and worked through. We have seen examples of success, where individuals and companies have faced these issues and developed solutions that work. We share some of these success examples in this book. The rewards of working through these problems can be significant increases in productivity, profitability, confidence, commitment, and, in general, better ways to live at work.

This book is about the transition we all face, as American business moves from the Industrial Age to the Information Age. At work today, change is underway. People are looking to better understand and cope with the change, and to prepare for the future. We believe this book will contribute to understanding why changes are happening, and point to actions that can lead to success in the future. Through a combination of storytelling, observation, and presentation of facts interwoven with the writings of other individuals, we hope to involve the reader in the story about transition in today's workplace.

This book takes a tour through some of our history, and some of the current conditions of the American workplace. This tour is meant to help us better understand where we are today and where we are headed.

We have given an entire chapter to the subject of diversity. Diversity already plays a major role in the economy, and its impact will grow with time.

Next we look at the how some companies have implemented programs and processes to improve their success, consistent with the needs of the Information Age. Then we look at the compelling case, and the challenges, for Small Business, and Independent Workers, which is where we believe most of the American workforce will end up, over time, in the Information Age.

Given the name of the book, we felt it appropriate to provide advice, in the form of rules for the transition to the Information Age. This advice is a summary of what we heard, observed, and what we personally believe will contribute to individual and company success. It is not rocket science, and much of it you may already know. The real advice is, pay attention and give the rules more than lip service, in order to be fully successful.

Finally, we close with Sarah's story, which is about accepting and embracing the changes necessary for success as an Independent Worker in the Information Age.

In the book you will find citations from interviews we conducted as part of our research. The interviews are presented without quotes and are re-creations, modified to protect the identity of the interviewees, who were all promised confidentiality. The information presented as part of the interview citations is accurate, taken from detailed interview notes, and when possible, re-validated with the original source.

We conducted interviews with companies, most of which are based in the Northeast. We focused on interviewing human resources executives. We looked for people who were recommended to us as doing good jobs or as being part of companies with good reputations both for work environment and for business success. Most of the interviews took place between 1993 and 1994. We focused on interviewing major companies, the top of the Fortune and Forbes 500 lists, because at the time, that is where we worked and the environment we most wanted to understand.

Since we began this project in 1992, we have both changed jobs. One of us has moved on to become an Independent Worker, and one of us continues to work in a large company environment.

We have both experienced and struggled with the challenges and opportunities presented in this book. We firmly believe that the American workplace is going through a radical transformation. We are optimistic about the potential these changes are unleashing all around us. We recognize the fear and frustration many currently experience related to work and changes that are underway. We hope this book, by contributing to an understanding of the need and reasons for change, will help to calm those fears and change frustration to optimism. We hope this book will contribute to an on-going dialog about how best to move forward, as individuals and as companies, to create a better workplace for all.

To the present! Make it work for you! To the future! May it be all that you hope for!

Acknowledgments

Our sincere gratitude to Professor Stuart Bruchey, who saw the importance of our work long before we recognized it ourselves. Our indebtedness to him for making it possible to share this work with others. Our many thanks to the patience of Robert McKenzie, our editor at Garland Publishing, who kept after us long past the point we thought we might never finish. And our thanks to all of the individuals who took time out of their busy schedules to share with us their views and stories. It is with the help of all of these people, that this book could come to be.

Andi & Gina

New Game, New Rules

I.
Where are we going?

This book looks at redefining the contract between company and individual. As we write, the marketplace is changing. Traditional ways of doing business are not working. The way companies and individuals interact can and must change, for the betterment of both.

This book is meant to do two things. First, we provide background to understand the need and urgency for changing the contract between company and individuals. Second, we provide insight on productively engaging in changes necessary to survive and prosper in today's and tomorrow's marketplace.

For companies, we provide suggestions on changing the relationship with employees to increase productivity, competitiveness and profitability. For individuals we provide insight into assessing a company's commitment (or lack of it) to its people, and a view of the alternatives to traditional employment. For both, we share a compelling picture of how work contracts are changing, and can change, in response to market forces.

WHAT'S HAPPENING AT WORK?

Today's workplace is undergoing a transformation.

History: Business is leaving the Industrial Age, entering the Information Age.

Corporate America: Traditional job roles and ways of managing are not delivering necessary performance increases.

Downsizing has taken a sizable toll on the quality of the workplace.

Diversity: Bias and barriers to access continue for women and minorities, despite the fact that our workforce grows ever more diverse.

Company Success: Forward thinking companies and individuals are searching for new ways to interact, to achieve business and personal goals.

Promotions: How individuals and companies handle the topic of promotions tells a great deal about them.

The Entrepreneurial Class: The loyalty contract between employees and companies has been severely tested.

Rules: Transitioning to the Information Age means Corporate America and the people working in it are playing a new game.

These are some indicators, symptoms of a radical shift in the way people go to work and the way companies do business.

CONDITIONS IN THE WORKPLACE

Take a closer look at these indicators of change in the workplace. These are forces that are driving change in our daily lives, and will forever change the way we view our work environment.

History

Business is leaving the Industrial Age, entering the Information Age.

We have a rich business history, which can serve us well through changes we encounter. American business has sought participation in the global market, and aggressively pursued the transition from manufacturing to service economy. Global market forces are driving changes at an ever increasing speed. Today's innovation is outdated by tomorrow. Yet both employees and companies are just beginning to work on the changes this forces in the way companies and individuals conduct business together.

Corporate America

Traditional job roles and ways of managing are not delivering necessary performance increases. Downsizing has taken a sizable toll on the quality of the workplace.

Companies are still trying to manage employees as if they were in a mass production, manufacturing economy. Employees are still looking for the structure of a production environment and the security of long term employment. Neither approach is likely to work in the changed, information oriented, global marketplace.

Both companies and employees are inseparably linked; what one does by definition affects the other. In the past 10 years, we have lived through very difficult times. Company downsizing results in distrust and survivor guilt in employees, leading to disengagement. Disengaged employees lead to under-productive companies, with under-performing results, leading to increased management pressure for greater output and frustration over undelivered goals. Suddenly it is no longer fun to go to work, and we begin to question why we keep trying.

Diversity

Bias and barriers to access continue for women and minorities, despite the fact that our workforce grows ever more diverse.

Sound financial advantages exist for embracing diversity at all levels of the organization, but American companies seem slow to develop methods and practices of inclusion.

We already have a diverse workforce, which will become even more diverse in the future. Either we can ignore the issues that go with diversity, or we can choose to find lasting solutions. Barriers to entry and to advancement for any individual will inhibit our competitive position in the global marketplace and in the Information Age. We must build the skills, starting with senior management, to include people with divergent backgrounds and points of view into a formerly cohesive environment.

Company Success

Forward thinking companies and individuals are searching for new ways to interact, to achieve business and personal goals.

Companies face enormous questions about why and how they exist, do business, make a profit, compete in the market. Employees' attitudes and expectations are changing. Employees once defined themselves by their job title: I am manager of . . . They must now define and defend their contribution to the bottom line: This year I was a member of several work teams which collectively delivered X . . . Both are looking for ways to increase agility and competitiveness in the marketplace.

Promotion

How individuals and companies handle the topic of promotions tells a great deal about them.

Choosing to consciously build tomorrow's workforce is likely to be one differentiator between highly successful companies and all others. Focus on people will become paramount as we come to understand that they are the foundation for all work.

The Entrepreneurial Class

The loyalty contract between employees and companies has been severely tested.

Perceived (and often real) loss of job security leaves questions about how productive and committed workers may be. Yesterday's superstars become tomorrow's outplaced executives, middle managers, supervisors, line-workers, janitors, and support staff. Companies are struggling with shedding excess workers and re-engaging those who stay. Employees are looking for new ways to participate to increase their control over their future in the workplace.

Traditional approaches to personal progression through a corporate hierarchy no longer apply, as corporations flatten and reach out for new skills. Individuals and companies once expressed concern about having too many employers appear on a resume. Both now learn to accept changes in employers every few years, or less.

A huge class of self-employed workers is emerging—with all sorts of backgrounds, skills, goals and income expectations. Growth of the American economy depends upon the success of this class.

Rules

Transitioning to the Information Age means Corporate America and the people working in it are playing a new game.

Companies and individuals are writing new rules about how they will interact with each other, about reasonable expectations for both parties. Using traditional approaches to work is like trying to play hockey using strategies and rules from wrestling.

This is an interesting and challenging time in American business history, and as the proverb goes, beware interesting times.

A CALL TO ACTION

Where do these indicators lead us? Companies and individuals can surely ignore changes that are taking place. For companies, it is very tempting to maintain they have no responsibility for solving their workers' problems. For individuals, it is very tempting to maintain that companies' problems are too big for them alone to solve. It is very tempting to take the easy way out and continue doing what worked before. After all, who expects their company to become the next version of a buggy whip maker.

A widening gap exists between employees and corporations. Companies focus on re-engineering and increasing profitability. Employees try to define where to fit and how to prosper in the new structure. Companies and employees may be at odds with each other, pursuing goals that may be mutually exclusive.

The Information Age is here to stay. Trying to force old models of management and employment onto the new marketplace is something like letting the genie out of the bottle, and then trying to put it back again. The marketplace will not revert to 1950 and the boom time of a high demand mass market. As we approach the year 2000, individual and company needs are fundamentally altered.

Today, individuals are wrestling with powerful negative issues at work, including:

- uncertainty about the future,
- frustration, sometimes leading to depression,
- general loss of trust in the companies for which they work,
- decreasing commitment, engagement and motivation, and
- concern about meeting personal goals such as security, getting ahead, making appropriate ethical choices, and caring for self and family.

At the same time, companies focus on major challenges including:

- engaging employees,
- addressing demographic changes in the workforce,
- finding the value of information,
- flattening organizational structures,
- achieving more than incremental gains in productivity,
- getting closer to the customer, and
- doing more with less.

For those individuals and companies willing to look long and hard at the way they do business, these are serious problems that they must face head on NOW.

WHAT TO LOOK FOR

We are constantly reminded that business comes down to the work of people. Singly and in groups, people perform the work.

People lay out tasks and goals. People create and carry out objectives and strategies. People consume goods and services.

We see companies of all sizes and types focusing on tasks and processes. In comparison to the focus on tasks and processes, we have seen relatively little time and effort invested in working with the most flexible asset in the workplace—people. For successful companies in the Information Age this will change. Focus on people will become paramount as we come to understand that they are the foundation for all work.

Real opportunity means having companies and individuals work together to find mutually supportive solutions to issues and challenges brought forward by transition to the Information Age.

> "Companies frequently give lip service to 'people' as the basic unit around which the company is organized. . . . Employees are frequently given token acknowledgment as the business's 'most important asset,' but their characteristics are then felt to vary too much or to be too unstable to serve as the real basis around which most corporate organizations can be planned.
> " . . . the organization planner is usually unable to adjust motivations and personalities to the requirements of the organization . . .
> "Unfortunately few organizations deal well with individual needs."[1]

Adapting to the Information Age requires a radical shift in traditional company views.

> "Jumping the curve means negotiating the transition from stressing mass and bulk to emphasizing brains and intelligence."[2]

In the Information Age, requiring employees to conform, or to work in an upwardly directed hierarchy represents a major liability. Tolerating a gulf between senior management and all others, is like having a millstone around the neck of organizations. Refusing to invest in development and training of the workforce equates to a significant competitive disadvantage. Penalizing risk takers results in loss of opportunity and speed, both critical success factors in the new age.

If you want to find models for success, Imparato and Harari, in their book *Jumping the Curve*,[3] recommend you look for risk takers. They advocate shifting from a traditional manufacturing and service delivery, to an economy of technology, in which information and speed of change are highly valued. Be willing to do what has not been done before. Believe that we are in an era of discovery, and that discovery is unpredictable. Recognize that clinging to the predictable will lead to greater chaos than embracing change.

Individuals will experience varying degrees of success depending upon their approach to security, risk, learning, work, structure. Companies can no longer supply such traditional staples as standard work hours and multi-layered promotions. Companies challenge their workers to build a new form of strength. To succeed at every level intellectual muscle instead of physical muscle will be required.

Change is inevitable. Unstoppable forces such as global markets, access to information, innovation and development are here to stay. Their impact is already felt, in downsizing, loss of vertical growth, speed of change, and a need to redefine security. These forces change individual and company relationships forever.

Today, opportunity exists to build a new contract between company and employee. Both parties can invest in each other's success. They will do so because they fully understand each other's needs, trust each other's motivations, see convergence in goals.

We are at a decisive point in our work history. Change will come at lightening speed. Opportunities will open up for those who are ready to grasp hold of them. Old rules will no longer work—nor will they hinder the progress of those previously left out. Opportunity exists to level the playing field, as information exceeds mass and capital accumulation as the tool on which to build success.

Once in our history, men and women of all races and creeds could combine physical strength with risk taking, hard work and dedication to get ahead. By doing so they could leap out of the circumstances to which they were born and achieve great successes. We have come to another such time and place. Intellectual muscle replaces physical muscle, computers replace pick and shovel, speed and responsiveness replace mass as success indicators.

This book, then, is about success—personal and company. It is about some things that can mark differences between success and failure. It is about understanding challenges that face us, such as lowering the stress and distress under which so many of us operate today. It is about opportunities that stand before all of us, to build intellectual muscle, to strike out in search of that which motivates each of us, individually and collectively. It is about acting cooperatively and collaboratively, to build an environment of trust and respect. It is about inclusion, regardless race, creed or nationality. It is about uniting family, business and personal goals into a whole that works.

II.
Historical Perspective

LEGACY OF ENTREPRENEURS

Prior to the Industrial Revolution, the United States had a rich history in what we today call entrepreneurship. Individuals rotated with the availability of work. They traded skills and physical strength for goods, services and income.

The United States also has a rich history of risk takers, who prized their freedom. Stories of The American Cowboy and of the Gold Rushes and Land Rushes are classic tales. These tales teach us about individuals who were willing to work hard and face frightening or difficult situations to follow their dreams.

Before the Industrial Revolution, individuals did work in the U.S., some as free men, some as indentured servants, some as slaves. Free men (and women), such as laborers and miners, followed the work. They were not tied to a single employer (unless they fell into a situation where expenses with an employer exceeded income and they had to stay with the employer to work off the debt.)

Indentured servants traded a period of servitude for learning a skill or trade. They often struck out on their own once the period of servitude was past. Once independent, they, too, maintained their independence.

In the slave community, they told stories of those who had escaped to freedom, and those who helped them to escape. People like Harriet Tubman (who helped organize the Underground Railroad) were, and still are, held up as heroes. Slaves were also known to buy their way to freedom. Then they moved on to places where they could be free to decide how and for whom they worked.

Our history is important as we move forward in the Information Age, again facing a time of entrepreneurship. It is good to know that our history has valued freedom and rewarded risk takers. In the Information Age, we will again see individual workers trading skills, and, this time, intellectual strength for goods services and income. Viewing freedom as 'good' will be valuable as individuals make the transition from a stable company environment, to transient, small and single-person work units.

THE DARK SIDE OF ENTREPRENEURSHIP

The independent workforce also faced significant problems at the beginning of the 20th Century.

> "Corporations became organizations that had a separate existence from the people involved with them; a company became an 'artificial being.' These organizations separated roles of manager and owner/investor and limited the liability of the investor. Money became as important as land . . . As the economy became more monetized, great concentrations of wealth developed."[1]

At the beginning of the 20th Century, workers had no job security, no collective bargaining, no child care, no benefits such as pensions, vacations, unemployment insurance health and dental care. These conditions contributed to a workforce that lived on the brink of disaster, one accident away from destitution. At that time, one major buffer between work and disaster was the family unit. Families of each generation tended to be large. Families stayed together in multi-generation support groups. Family members generally assumed the obligations of caring for each other.

Independent workers at the beginning of the Information Age face problems similar to those stated above. However, today's workforce is much less likely to have the buffer of extended family, as existed at the beginning of the 20th Century. If the U.S. workforce is to move confidently into the Information Age, people must be able to step back from the brink of disaster. They must be able to build distance between themselves and potential financial tragedy.

Problems of the early 20th Century, recast for the Information Age, represent both challenge and opportunity. They cannot be ignored. These problems are especially acute in small businesses, which now account for 99% of the net new jobs in the U.S. The solutions will influence the behavior and quality of our workforce for many years to come.

JOB SECURITY

As jobs become shorter term, and workers move from one project to the next, their security is based upon their marketable skills. It will be much more difficult to reside within the company, to earn income for holding a position rather than delivering an outcome.

Comments regarding the latest downsizing at AT&T:
"She (one AT&T employee who accepted the latest buyout) added: 'You always read about another company laying people off and you have to be cognizant that you could be next. It's a useful paranoia'
". . . another benefit consultant, said: ' it should be a wake-up call. You need to keep your skill sets in line with the needs of your industry, or else.' . . .
"AT&T, with more than $75 billion in annual revenue, has cut an average of nearly 900 employees, about the size of a medium-sized business, *every month* for the (last) 12 years . . . That comes to 126,000 jobs."[2]

Downsizing has challenged the notion of job security. Once secure managers now find themselves out of work. Those still employed wonder whether they will be next in line for the loss of jobs. To many people, there seems to be little reason why one person is out of a job and another co-worker stays.

People must form a new definition of security, based upon flexibility, matching of personal skills with marketplace needs and commitment to constant learning. Refusal to change will result in being left behind in the race for jobs, income and opportunity.

BARGAINING FOR WORK AND BENEFITS

Changes are taking place throughout the work environment in the way people and groups bargain for work and for benefits. These changes affect the way we define jobs, the way we protect ourselves in case of health care needs, and the way we negotiate for benefits in general.

Bargaining For Work

As individuals move from project to project and company to company, collective bargaining is likely to move further and further into the background. Bargaining with companies will be based upon individual skills, company needs and project requirements.

Individuals have built negotiating skills in recent times, as a result of growth in white collar work, development of a supervisory/managerial class, and fall-off in union representation. Individuals at all levels of organizations have learned to interview for jobs, negotiate salary and raises, define a job description. These skills help newly independent workers and small business owners in bargaining for work, goods and services.

Union Bargaining

Changes have already been noted in union approaches to collective bargaining.

> "The wide range of options open to employers to relocate, restructure, reorganize, and redefine work in the midst of a worldwide economic slowdown has made it necessary for unions to change their traditional adversarial tactics. Mass production ushered in the era of strong unions and plentiful, steady jobs. Lean production and 'just in time' inventory control are designed to reduce the number of steady jobs. . . .
>
> "Between 1979 and 1989 membership in the (UAW) union fell by 500,000, about a third of its total."[3]

Bargaining For Benefits

Moving forward, one area that will benefit from collective bargaining is the provision of benefits. Typically, unions (for unionized workers) and companies (for non-union workers) negotiated benefits for the workforce. It is common practice for unions and companies to negotiate and oversee administration of:

- health care and dental care insurance plans
- investments (401K plans, stock plans and pension funds)
- vacation accrual and payout
- child care and elderly care spending accounts
- calculation and payment of bonuses
- collection and filing with the government of federal, state and local taxes, social security premiums and unemployment insurance

New Collective Bargaining Units

Lobbying firms, cooperatives and middle men are forming to address benefit problems. National Small Business United, a Washington, D.C.-based organization, has as one of its objectives to form insurance buying cooperatives in states throughout the U.S., for the benefit of small businesses.

One barrier they cite is that state law currently governs insurance, rather than national standards. As a result, it is both time consuming and expensive to set up cooperatives on a state by state basis. They are proceeding, however, working directly to form cooperatives in some states, working with insurance companies in other states, and pressing for national standards at the federal level.

Companies are also entering the market, to address the need for high quality flexible workers, and to manage and administer employee benefit programs. There are increasing numbers of examples of companies which are emerging as middlemen. These middlemen contract to take over some portion of a client company's workforce. The middlemen hire workers onto their payroll on an extended basis, often providing workers with a full range of benefits. This means that workers are employed by the middlemen, while working for the client companies.

The advantage for the client companies is that they now have the flexibility of a contingency workforce. They can get people when then need them and let them go without obligations when then don't. The best of the workers may be able to continue working for the middlemen, past the end of the 'job' at the client company, by accepting assignment to another client company. In such a case, by working through the middleman, workers may be able to maintain continuity of benefits and income, while working on a project basis and shifting from one 'employer' to another.

The client company pays a premium to the middleman, but that is still less than the costs of testing, hiring, training, benefits and severance, which are now the responsibility of the middleman.

Skilled, conscientious employees are rewarded with the opportunity for continued employment and stable benefits. The middlemen, by supplying a market need, are able to create a market niche, generating revenue for their services.

HEALTH CARE

We met George through business. One day our conversation moved to the subject of changing jobs. George had a story to tell about the intangible holds companies may have on their workforce—whether they realize it, or not.

George had been a partner at a Philadelphia firm for many years. He and his wife, Nancy, wanted to move to New York. The children were grown and gone. George and Nancy had visions of a new phase to their lives: work in one of the greatest cities in the world, an apartment off Gramercy Park, Sunday's spent at art galleries and museums. To fulfill the dream, George had worked hard to find the right job offer with a firm in New York, and he had done it. George began.

> I can remember the day as clearly as if it were this morning. It was a Friday. We planned to take off from work for the afternoon, take the train to New York. I was going to meet with the new firm and negotiate the final terms of the new job offer. Nancy had a doctor's appointment in the morning, and when she was through, she would call and we would meet at the train station.
> Nancy called, as expected, but she had terrible news. The Doctor found a lump in her breast, and wanted her to go for more tests immediately. Suddenly everything else was on hold.
> I called the firm in New York, made an excuse, and delayed the meeting. A few days later, Nancy was on to surgery, then chemotherapy. I never took the job in New York. I could not afford to.

What happened to Nancy would be, by insurance standards, a 'preexisting condition' at the new firm. We would not have coverage of the expenses related to Nancy's cancer for at least 12 months. Sure, I could get COBRA (Consolidated Omnibus Budget Reconciliation Act) coverage for 18 months from my old firm. But what if other things happened to Nancy, and the new firm's insurance plan did not provide full coverage? It was a much smaller firm, and the burden of medical costs on their insurance plan would be felt. What if their premiums went up because of what was happening to Nancy. Or even worse, what if the insurance company canceled us, or the whole firm's plan, because of the costs?

I finally explained the situation to the firm in New York. We agreed to let the job offer drop. Nancy and I stayed in Philadelphia. Fortunately, today, Nancy is okay, but we will never look at health care coverage the same way! In some ways, though, I feel lucky. What if I did not have this job in Philadelphia to fall back on?[4]

We believe that lack of portability, and inequality of health care benefits have created a barrier to movement of workers from one employer to another. Employees with extensive health care plans think twice, and three times, about moving on. Companies which heavily subsidize their benefit plans are more attractive employers, after, and sometimes before, considering specifics of job and salary offer. Waivers of preexisting conditions, limited premiums, deductions and co-payments, health care spending accounts to shelter pretax dollars, and coverage no matter the nature of the illness or expense, have been hallmarks of large company health care plans.

Once out of large companies, individuals pay higher premiums for health care, assuming they have no preexisting conditions and can obtain coverage. Younger workers and families may choose to forego insurance premiums, assuming that with youth goes health, and trusting that accidents will not happen or that someone else's insurance plan will cover them.

It is estimated that more than 20% of the population today has no health care coverage. According to the Survey of Small and Mid-Sized Businesses[5], 11% of respondents (companies with less than 500 employees) do not offer any standard benefits. Leading the way in offering no standard benefits were companies with 0-19 employees.

The lack of affordable health care insurance is truly a disaster waiting to happen. Consider that one day of hospital care can exceed a week's pay, and a few days in intensive care can equate to months of wages. How can we expect workers to bear this burden alone, no matter how independent they might be?

Small companies are at a competitive disadvantage versus large companies. They face higher premiums for less coverage, undergo frequent (sometimes yearly) changes in providers, and lack sufficient depth to self insure to reduce costs.

RETIREMENT PLANS

Our workforce is aging, and it is not prepared to provide for its needs throughout the 'golden years' of retirement. Nor do tax laws provide sufficient incentives to motivate change. The Baby Boom generation is on a collision course with old age.

Pension Plans And Retirement Savings

As individuals leave or lose secure employment situations, they wrestle with loss of benefits. If the company offers a pension plan, individuals may be forced out prior to retirement age, with little or no benefits.

> "Mr. Bowers, 48, doesn't qualify for a full
> pension. Typically an AT&T manager would have to
> be 55, with 20 years of service, to qualify. There is
> always the pension he will receive after working for
> 10 years at Allied Chemical, about $300 a month.
>   'Enough to buy a loaf of bread in the year
> 2009,' Mr. Bowers said ruefully."[6]

One exception is the worker nearing retirement and able to capitalize on an early retirement offer. Although, even with a buyout, one should carefully evaluate all retirement benefits, working with an expert, to assess the impact of leaving early.

> "The bigger surprise can be in pension benefits.
> A 56-year-old bank executive . . . considered taking
> a buyout to move to a higher-paying job . . . .But Mr.
> Altfest (the banker's financial planner) calculated
> that the banker would lose $300,000 in pension
> benefits. The banker stayed put."[7]

Many companies today have eliminated pension plans in favor of 401K plans, putting the burden of retirement planning and investment squarely onto the individual's shoulders. Once out of the company, individuals may forego retirement planning, as they struggle to pay living expenses, college expenses, taxes.

Retirement Savings For Small Business Owners

This is another area of concern for the long term health of the American economy. The average small business owner makes $32,000 per year. Will small business owners make significant investments in retirement savings plans? When trading off today's survival versus meeting retirement needs sometime in the future, probably not.

As the number of independent workers and small business owners continues to grow, the likelihood is high that many of them are not financially well prepared for retirement. If left unaddressed, this will result in growing down line pressure on the Social Security system, as individuals enter retirement with little or no personal assets. Long term, the American retirement system will benefit if we create incentives for retirement savings, and ease administration through simplified regulations.

CHILD CARE

Child care responsibility continues to fall disproportionately on the shoulders of women. Issues surrounding child care include long enough hours to allow for commuting, reliability and safety, need for part time work in order to spend time with the children, finding care when children are sick. These issues contribute to lower wage levels that some women continue to endure as compared to their male counterparts.

> "Women have always taken care of children other than their own, sometimes for long periods of time as foster or adoptive parents. This kind of labor has tended to be invisible, as if child care was not work; especially if the woman had her own children, observers sometimes imagine that a few more make no difference. In fact, child care is not only difficult but also skilled labor. The need for it has expanded directly in proportion to increases in the number of women in the labor force, and the supply is never adequate. But, in a vivid example of how the market does not work—how increased demand for labor does not raise wages—the earnings of child-care givers remain at the absolute bottom of the wage scale, often even below the minimum wage. This is both because their customers, working mothers, simply cannot afford higher wages and because the workers are usually those without access to better jobs.

> "Day care for working women is highly
> stratified. The most privileged employed women use
> not-for-profit day care centers or individual in-home
> babysitters. Most women workers rely on friends and
> relatives. Those who can't are likely to use family
> daycare, which usually means women taking
> children into their own homes for low fees, or
> commercial daycare centers."[8]

Women are not about to return to the home; their place in the workforce is firmly established. As American business moves forward, in order to increase commitment and productivity, finding reliable solutions for child care is essential.

Building tomorrow's workforce is now in the hands of millions of child care providers. With such individuals and institutions, our children receive varying levels of security, education, nutrition and health care. These experiences not only affect today's parents, but will also impact the competitive abilities of the U.S. workforce in the future. Today's children will enter the workforce, in total, in less than 25 years.

The old proverb, an ounce of prevention is worth a pound of cure, surely applies to child care. Solutions to child care needs can free today's workforce from nagging concerns that decrease focus and result in days off from work. Solutions to child care needs can contribute to an early head start for this next generation.

LEGACY OF THE INDUSTRIAL AGE

> "It is sometimes said that the United States has
> been entering a postindustrial era since the end of
> World War II, that it is now best described as an
> 'information economy.' If so, this would represent

the most recent in a series of fundamental changes in
the structure of the American economy."[9]

The Industrial Age changed the way a major portion of the
population was taught to work. Conformity, following rules,
viewing workers as replaceable, routinizing jobs, deskilling
workers, are all part of the work legacy from the Industrial Age.

"Between 1880 and 1920 the U.S. population
doubled. The number of factory workers more than
tripled.

". . . Turnover rates and absenteeism were
astronomical by today's standards. The Amoskeag
Co.'s textile mills, in Manchester, N.H. had to hire
24,000 in one year to maintain a labor force of
13,700. Ford Motor Co.'s Highland, Mich. plant,
incredibly, had to hire 54,000 over 12 months to
maintain 13,000 employees. . . . (Finding) 10% (of
workers) out every day—was more or less standard
in the years preceding World War I.

". . . Between 1910 and 1920 the ranks of
supervisory employees grew nearly two and a half
times as fast as the ranks of wage earners."[10]

Mass markets required deskilled workers who could follow
rules and would not challenge processes. Workers were
replaceable, and continuity came from managers, who were
supposed to be the repository of information and process control.
Managers were invested with the knowledge of what work was to
be done, and how. Workers were supposed to follow directions as
given. A gap arose, between 'us' and 'them', separating worker
and supervisor/manager. In recent times, as inevitable economic
downturns came about, the gaps between 'us' and 'them'
widened.

". . . managerialism promoted an elite. It
emphasized the distinction between members of a
managerial class and others, including employees
and customers. It isolated value-added knowledge

within the ranks of senior management and
corporate staff. It generated a culture where
managers presumed to speak not only for themselves
but also for other constituencies, particularly
shareholders. It also promoted the value of
generalists whose talent was in working the
bureaucracy rather than in providing understanding
of the product or customer needs.

"Now, however, managerialism is exhausted. It
has degenerated to a set of operating principles and
business priorities that no longer fit the current stage
of social and business development. In a world
where controls are increasingly decentralized,
managerialism is the ideology of the power to
control others. It emphasizes size at a time when
scale appears less relevant than innovation. . . . It
promotes 'me first' individualism at a time when
productivity depends on teams and alliances. . . .
Managerialism is grounded in a search for order and
stability in a business world that is becoming more
unruly and ephemeral."[11]

WEALTH AND INFLATION

"After showing no clear trend toward
concentration before 1820, nonhuman wealth
(excluding ownership of slaves as a form of wealth)
became much more concentrated across the
nineteenth century as skilled labor, professional
groups, and urban wealthholders prospered much
faster than farm hands, and the urban unskilled.
Earnings and total incomes became even more
markedly unequal between the 1890s and the First
World War, leveled dramatically but briefly during
the war, and resumed the trend toward inequality in
the 1920s.

". . . The legislation (of the Reagan era, based
upon supply side economics) did bring about a

redistribution of income—from the poor and the middle class to the better-off segments of society."[12]

"As many learned, inflation damages the values that hold a society together. Speculation, consumption, and self-indulgence push aside trust, diligence, and hard work. People become inordinately concerned with how much they make and less concerned with what they do. . . . Jealousies and feelings of entitlement encumber productive relationships."[13]

One of Reagan's priorities was the conquest of inflation.

"Unfortunately, there also occurred an unanticipated drop in the velocity of money in the early 1980s, and partly for this reason the nation was plunged into the longest and deepest recession since the Great Depression."[14]

Inflation, price increases and other related economic pressures have led to significant problems in the workplace and at home. Individuals and companies struggle to survive financially and to exceed break even. Emphasis is placed on doing what needs to be done to stay employed. Loyalty, trust, commitment are lost in the face of downsizings and financial struggles, as the Industrial Age ends.

"The global economic system prizes the efficient production of goods more than the dignity of human beings."[15]

Interestingly, the Information Age represents an opportunity to break through many of the very issues that are coming to the fore because of the decline of the Industrial Age.

TRANSITION TO THE INFORMATION AGE

Opportunity exists today to recreate the workplace, thanks to the emergence of the Information Age. Size and capital access are no longer the constraints they once were on business start up. Conformity is no longer an advantage. A minority woman, today, can potentially open and sustain a business start up with a $5,000 credit card line of credit.

Opportunity exists to build lasting business relationships based upon trust and attention to detail. As we shift from building mass and profiting from decreases in unit costs, to building organizational competence and focusing on customer needs one customer at a time, we are likely to see a return to core human values as well.

> ". . . the promise that information technology has for creating a world of extraordinary prosperity begins with resolving age-old concerns about human relationships and personal responsibility."[16]

> "Since the 1960s a major structural change has been taking place in the world economy. Access to capital, technological knowledge, and innovations, and global channels of sales and marketing, . . . has permitted an international rationalization of the location of production to take place. The globe is thus becoming a single marketplace, with goods being made wherever they can be produced the cheapest. . . . In addition, the availability of data processing machines, microprocessors, and satellite communications facilities has made it possible for manufacturers to divide the process of production into separate operations that can be performed at different sites and then integrated into a single product."[17]

Even in global markets, size does not equate to success.

"GM and IBM are prime examples of how size does not guarantee success or even survival. Giant companies that have controlled substantial shares of the world market have sustained gargantuan losses in recent years. The competition from smaller firms sharpens as the technology and know-how to develop transnational enterprises become cheaper and more widely available. Because incremental technological changes come so fast and have such an unpredictable impact on the market in electronics, drugs and computers, for example, even within the largest firms with long track records and deep roots in many countries, there is a growing sense of impermanence."[18]

SUSTAINABLE VALUE-ADD

As we move out of the Industrial Age, it is important to remember that economies of scale and scope worked in America because of the size of the market (lowering unit costs requires mass markets). As demand has slowed, and variety of goods and services has increased, along with diversity of the population, value-added strategies are reaping real rewards. Companies are using value-added strategies to attract and retain customers and to differentiate themselves, contributing to their success in the market. The ability to create a business driven by sustainable value-add strategies and actions will be a major differentiator for highly successful companies in the Information Age.

". . . in the 1970s and 1980s, value-added strategies increasingly (became) the norm. The intertwining of globalization processes, and the trade liberalization, communication technologies, and transportation advances that accompanied it, changed the game. Given the new level and intensity of competition and customer expectations, the old rules no longer applied."[19]

Value-added strategies used by a few companies to differentiate themselves in the 1970s and 1980s provide clues to success qualities for the Information Age. Qualities such as zero defects, customized/personalized products and services, innovation and variety have helped companies to pull ahead of their competitors. These qualities help companies get close to customers, and understand opportunities. Companies with these qualities seem more able to more quickly develop products and deliver services, to meet specific and differing needs.

When discussing the benefit of value-add strategies, it is important to point out what we believe can drive sustainable value-add and what cannot.

We believe successful value-add, which is sustained over time, comes from willingness to see the world from the customer's point of view. Desire to listen and willingness to respond contribute to sustainable value-add, as does follow-through to problem resolution, until things are right according to the customer. We believe that sustainable value-add comes from fundamental willingness to see problems as opportunities, and obstacles as things which make us stronger and better than we would otherwise have been.

We do not believe that value-add results in, nor is it sustained by, an excuse to charge an excessive profit margin. Someone else is likely to find an opportunity to exploit the margin, and the competitive advantage is quickly lost. Sustainable value-add represents an opportunity to differentiate a product or service provider by providing a better product or service at equal or near equal pricing.

Sustainable value-add does not mean remaking something that already exists into something only slightly better. Anyone can tinker, and deliver incremental improvements. Sustainable value-add does mean creating something substantially new or different, leveraging current knowledge and developments to achieve more than incremental changes.

Sustainable value-add is founded on open information systems and the people who use them. These open systems are used by risk takers. These risk takers are committed to continual learning. They use information and learning to meet individual customer needs even before customers may understand their own need. These, then, are skills to be prized in the Information Age.

III.
Corporate America Is Changing

Something is happening. But what? The labels include, 'the anxious class,' 'continuous downsizing,' 'shift to a service economy,' 'matrix management,' 'team based approach,' 'work as temporary assignments,' 'the entrepreneurial workforce,' 'rightsizing for tomorrow.'

People are out of jobs. Or are they? Companies are changing size, shape, scope, and the result is people's work lives are changing as well. The dependable work front, a staple of people's lives, seems much less dependable.

Companies must go through a process of continual change and renewal if they are to survive in today's competitive marketplace. The skills and tasks needed yesterday are different from those needed today, and will change even more by tomorrow.

Employees want control over their future. The 'X Generation' does not feel the commitment to major corporations that their Baby Boom successors felt. Baby Boomers are not enjoying the forty-year, single-employer careers of their parents.

On the other hand, employing individuals out of benevolence is not the answer. One needs only look as far as IBM, General Motors, and the telephone companies, to name a few. These organizations are trying desperately to streamline, to reduce workforce size, to focus. Keeping employees in functions long after the need for the function has passed, is not the answer. Lifetime employment contracts, and refusal to move people on have resulted in bloated payrolls, excessive costs to take products to market, uncompetitive pricing, and loss of focus on doing things 'easier, faster, better'.

"Like many other companies, AT&T has been steadily paring the number of employees to cut costs. But unlike other companies, AT&T is doing so not because it is losing money—it is expected to post a profit of \$5.6 billion this year—but because it is trying to escape its bloated past. . . .

"AT&T is the largest profitable company to choose a more or less permanent state of revolution, in which it may rapidly add jobs, either piecemeal or through acquisitions, and years later just as rapidly shed jobs in a gigantic, nerve-jangling (for employees, at least) work in progress."[1]

The contract of employer as benevolent caretaker is gone. Or, more likely, the contract is being rewritten, to include employer, management and worker as equally responsible and able parties. We see ourselves, and those around us, expressing concern about our relationships with our employers. We are all asking questions about where we fit. We want to know how best to continue, using the tools and skills we have worked so hard to assemble.

The workforce is increasingly diverse. Age, gender, race, culture, environment all influence how we look, act and contribute. Learning to work together, respecting differences and encouraging collaboration, are both challenges and opportunities.

"The academic research literature indicates that on one hand, individuals in problem-solving situations are usually most comfortable when they interact with people who are like themselves. On the other hand, the best solutions to ambiguous, complex, nonroutine problems—the norm in today's business world—are generated by groups with heterogeneous membership. Thus, once again, it would make sense to create an organization where people with diverse skills and backgrounds can understand and work well with one another. . . .

"When diverse groups and individuals within an organization hold a commitment to shared vision and values, coherence and control emerge, and diversity of people and ideas becomes a powerful competitive weapon."[2]

Change is truly underway. With change come choice and opportunity. We, as workers, managers, business owners and stockholders, have choices to make. We can choose to stay where we are, and wait for change to overtake us. Or, we can make use of change to further our dreams. We can use change to create something better than what we have at work today.

DEBUNKING OLD STEREOTYPES

Old rules are broken. New ones are just being written. Employment for most of one's career is no longer likely to be within a single company. Perhaps employment is no longer likely to be within a company at all, in traditional terms. Some consider employment for five years or more within the same company to be an accomplishment. They make jokes that if you have not been fired at least once you have not yet arrived as a business person.

According to both President Clinton and Labor Secretary Robert Reich, the American worker can expect to have eight different jobs during their career.[3]

As Robert Tomasko wrote in *Rethinking the Corporation*,[4] we are challenging companies' old ways of thinking. No longer can we make assumptions such as:

- small companies cannot compete
- going outside for services is a weakness
- individual performers are the basis of company success
- deskilling workers by putting them in boxes is good

- a manager not in control is not doing his or her job
- information is sacred, access is limited to those with a 'right' to know
- becoming a manager is a growth goal

A fundamental shift taking place in Corporate America, challenges these assumptions, and many more, which we once took for granted.

Small Companies Can Compete!

With the Information Age, we move past the time when substantial plant and equipment investments are needed to compete on a unit cost basis. Unit costs no longer count in the same way as before, thanks to a world of mass customization. Micro computers and home-based office workers replace plant and equipment.

> "Ironically it is the computer itself that will help reconcile those ancient opposites, technology and humanism. . . . computers strip away the mechanical, repetitive, soul-destroying elements of work. . . . Left are the most essentially human tasks: sensing, judging, creating, building human relationships."[5]

As skilled middle managers are downsized, one logical outlet for their substantial experience is in small companies in which they can play a principal role. With nearly all net job formation in the U.S. economy coming from companies with less than 100 employees, small companies must be achieving some significant measure of success.

Going Outside For Services Is A Strength!

Manufacturing companies struggled throughout the 1980s to increase machine productivity and shed wasted effort. Service companies, too, sought to flatten their organizations, reengineer processes and turn over an expensive, mature workforce. Companies upgraded equipment, merged with more productive companies, or shut their doors. The net of all of this effort has been to clear away much of the nonessential services companies previously performed as they went about their daily business.

Reengineering is underway in some form and scope in 70% of 600 large U.S. and European businesses, and under consideration in half of the remaining 30%.[6] Mail room, computer departments and cafeterias are only a few of the targets for moving business out. As companies focus on core services, and 'getting back to basics,' opportunities exist for small companies to step in and create themselves around service offerings that relieve their larger counterparts of non-essential or burdensome work.

Team Members Are The Basis Of Company Success!

Teams become the basic building blocks of companies. Managers struggle to participate rather than dominate. People learn to respect and support participants' varying contributions.

> "No one today would seriously question the need for greater participation of everyone in an organization, with all moving to higher and higher levels of responsibility and performance. The question for the leader is how to accomplish this involvement within the framework of traditionally maintained roles. The answer is that it can't be done. Something has to give."[7]

Team members learn to speak up, question, identify problems, solutions and options, own the process.

> "In the mindset created by the next-generation companies, the roles and obligations and expectations prescribed by conventional corporate pyramids go out the window. . . . That elusive goal, a company in which everyone thinks like an owner, becomes part of everyday life.[8]"

Teams that are focused, fully empowered and self-directed are the most powerful. They definitely outpace their individual counterparts through the strength of collaboration. They deliver more broad-based solutions. They can respond to the need to deliver customer-specified products and services, and innovations, on-time, ahead of budget.

Deskilling Workers By Putting Them In Boxes Is Bad!

In service companies, there are few assets outside the workforce. In manufacturing companies, the workforce is the company's most flexible tool. It is unlikely that machines can manage all tasks, talk to customers, co-workers and suppliers, investigate problems and opportunities, and work through to value-added solutions.

> "Every one of the ten most common reengineering mistakes listed by Michael Hammer and Steven Stanton in . . . The Reengineering Revolution . . ., involves managers who ignored . . . issues like leadership, courage and 'the concerns of your people'."[9]

We cannot afford to lose the contribution of our workforce as we seek to define our place in the global, information driven world of the 21st Century.

A Manager Not In Control Is Doing His Or Her Job!

"Thus managers are used to experiencing their own power only in terms of control: control over resources, information, and people. They keep control by keeping other people powerless; to them, power is a zero-sum game. This is a notion of the organization that has held for thousands of years, and despite the fact that such exercise of power may be counterproductive today, it is far from extinct.

". . . Operating an organization by letting go of control and trusting the people below you to come through is a difficult proposition at first. Yet the new form of power—empowerment—means that people in organizations must do so. As a result, the organization will begin to gain the help of people by their voluntary commitment, not through fear and compulsion.

". . . The real power in the new organization belongs not so much to the people in high positions as to the people who make things happen, who are able to mobilize themselves to get things done, and who inspire others to work with them."[10]

Information Is Sacred, Access Should Be For Everyone!

Limiting information flow limits analysis, diversity of problem identification and solution presentation, speed of response and buy-in to process.

In *Open the Doors, Tell the Truth,* Oren Harari tells about being on an airplane flight with serious mechanical problems. The pilot openly talked about the crisis with the passengers, almost constantly, until they were again safely on the ground. The pilot's willingness to communicate changed Harari's response to the situation from fear to 'calm and focused.'

Because of the experience, Harari became a devoted customer of the airline, SAS. He also reflected on the value of open information flow.

> "I believe that one of the most self-defeating actions managers can take these days is to work behind closed doors, literally and figuratively. Closed doors inevitably yield a culture of secrecy, 'for your eyes only' information hoarding, and sugarcoated partially true communication to those outside. Among the 'insiders,' closed doors create the delusion that they are in control and in the know, and that their decisions will be quickly understood and eagerly endorsed by those outside. Among the 'outsiders', closed doors generate the kind of paranoid fantasies that can paralyze an organization. . . . Closed doors, not surprisingly, create a workforce that feels powerless, alienated from the ultimate decisions, and skeptical about the veracity of the communications—and the communicator—thereafter."[11]

Probably the most prominent symbol of the Information Age is the personal computer. Computers can open and speed information flow and analysis. Computers, and the information systems which run on them, must be accessible to people at all levels of the organization, with few restrictions. Otherwise, companies simply churn through unusable data faster, and further frustrate employees who suspect the information is there but who cannot see it.

> "The personal computer is the most powerful definer of new work. In contrast to mainframe, which centralized information, personal computer systems are networked, and local units can call up centralized data at will. This kind of system has tremendous power. . . . Access to information breaks down the barriers and gives people more control over their work.

> "But in order to use these new systems and make the best use of data, people need freedom to take action. New accounting and information systems must begin with the assumption that people at any point in the organization may need instantaneous information to be able to take action."[12]

Becoming A Manager Is Not Necessarily A Growth Goal!

We are at a decisive point in our work history. More people than ever are presenting themselves as middle (and senior) manager candidates. The shrinking number of jobs in Corporate America cannot satisfy all these expectant candidates.

The Baby Boom generation boosts the size of the bulging middle management group. More people than ever are in their early 40's and up—standard timing for reaping the rewards which Corporate America has traditionally offered.

PRESSURE, PRESSURE, PRESSURE

Opportunity exists today to rewrite rules, to change definitions of success, progress, well-being. To move forward, however, understanding the barriers created by responses to change is important. As we learn new ways to think and act in the workplace, we must also be aware of the pressures confronting all levels of workers.

> ". . . internal concerns (existed) about how work was to be done in GE's (General Electric Co.) newly flatted pyramid. While many middle managers accepted intellectually the need for Welch's changes to ensure the corporation's global competitiveness, they also felt mounting pressures about doing their own jobs well.

". . . management layers (can be) removed but
the net result may well be the conversion of the
company into a corporate pressure cooker."[13]

Customers continue to press to obtain similar or better
services at lower prices. To protect margins, companies want
greater productivity from every asset they hold. A primary target
for protecting and increasing margins is the workforce. Pressure
is on companies to squeeze greater output from the workforce, at
the same or lower cost, to protect profit margins.

This pressure shows up in a variety of ways.

"We're all still trying to get our stories straight
in the new workplace. For example: Let's say
management embraces the idea of a more
collaborative workplace, but in the meantime insists
that people make their numbers even as they learn
the new system.

". . . the pressure is palpable, tempers are,
deadlines are missed, and nights and weekends are
spent working. People start telling themselves they
must just be incompetent for not making the
numbers, or lazy for not clocking 60 hours. What
should they be telling themselves? Says Tobey
(organizational development consultant Linda
Tobey): 'This is crazy.'

"Hearing people talk like that, she suggests, is
healthy. Not hearing people talk is a bad sign.
'There's a kind of panicky quiet inside of the storm,'
says Tobey. 'People get so overwhelmed they no
longer know what to say.'"[14]

CHANGES IN VALUES AND PRIORITIES

The Information Age is here to stay. Its changes are all
around us, already. Traditional rewards of a stable workplace—

steady increases in income, job security, opportunity for promotions—are missing.

Former trappings of success—progress through the ranks at corporate, pursuing the corner office—are gone. Demands to justify job and contribution value are high, and increasing, as companies move to lower costs and protect margins.

> "Employee needs, customer wants and owner requirements all must be kept in some sort of balanced state."[15]

A major challenge is finding equilibrium between customer, owner and employee. Even more complicated is doing so while moving through imbalances and imperfections that are part of the transition from Industrial Age to Information Age.

To get close to customers, companies move decision making out of corporate headquarters. To control costs, companies cut headquarters staff and freeze salaries. Individuals continue to pursue 'promotions to corporate' as part of the process of getting ahead. They pursue salary increases in order to keep up with cost of living increases. However, these usual trappings of success have now become tickets to front row seats at the next downsizing party.

In an article in *Fortune*, Ken Labich quotes Ross Webber, chair of the management department at the Wharton School of the University of Pennsylvania:

> "There's been a change in the myths that talented people in this new generation guide their lives by, and an entrepreneurial, rather than corporate, connection is a strong part of that mythology.[16]"

Labich further states,

> "As recently as 1990, a quarter of Columbia University's new MBAs joined large manufacturers; last year just 13% did so. At Stanford nearly 70% of

the business school's class of '89 joined big
companies, defined as those with more than 1,000
employees. In 1994 only about half did so."[17]

Individuals may choose to stay closer to customers. This
means staying out in the field. It also means staying away from
headquarters, the former center of power and balance in corporate
life. As ever more headquarters staff are downsized, moving to
corporate has less value, greater risk.

Companies now have fewer and fewer openings to use to
move employees into headquarters, from the field. Consequently,
a key means is lost to instill corporate values and build
relationships among future senior managers. The field, a
traditional starting point for careers, is now becoming an end
game, as employee and company work to get and stay close to
customers.

Customer tolerance for bearing headquarters overhead costs
is gone. As customers seek to incrementalize pricing, selecting
carefully those items or services for which they will and will not
agree to pay, every overhead expense comes into question.
Opposing needs put pressure on both individuals and companies:
for companies to decrease costs over time, for individuals to
increase income over time.

> "The world is at an historic crossroads.
> Everything is under challenge. . . . To succeed in the
> future, managers will have to bring a taste for
> innovation to organizations that have longed for
> predictability; an emphasis on brains instead of mass
> and size; a priority for coherence in the face of
> segmentation and disorganization; and a spirit of
> responsibility to replace expedient and self-serving
> attitudes."[18]

Thanks to customer demands for lower costs, and
competitive pressures, companies ask employees to continuously
justify their expense by delivering results. Companies are less

willing to put forth promotions, which add to hierarchy and increase costs for the same worker. Growing hierarchy and increasing costs are in direct opposition to today's objectives of flattening structures and reducing costs. Reward for work well done, and loyalty to the company has become much less tangible—and much less reliable.

BABY BOOMERS

Now the Baby Boom generation has hit a most expensive bubble. Baby Boomers are mature, experienced, expensive and in too plentiful supply. Companies do not need as many tenured, experienced workers as the Baby Boom generation supplies in its waning days. The Baby Boom generation is battling within its ranks for limited seniority positions.

Just as the number of middle manager candidates peaks, thanks to the Baby Boom generation, the critical need for middle managers falls off thanks to the Information Age. This is not unlike having a buggy whip factory in full production, only to find that the automobile does not need buggy whips. Refashioning the output, in this case middle managers, is possible, but it is not easy.

Besides more people presenting themselves at the doorstep of middle management than ever before, they arrive with more education than ever before. The post World War II emphasis on high school diplomas and technical and college degrees, fuels this surge.

"In the two decades between 1947 and 1968 employment in services grew ten times as fast (as manufacturing) and brought about a massive shift from blue-collar work, including farming, to white-collar work, especially in professional, technical and clerical jobs. Increasingly high levels of educational attainment accompanied these developments. In

contrast to the prewar period, high school graduation
became common among the young, with rising
proportions of both men and women going on to
college. The number of bachelor degrees granted
doubled between 1966 and 1974, with master's
degrees and doctorates increasing at nearly the same
rate."[19]

Education is good—in fact necessary for success in the
Information Age. However, the traditional use of education has
been to secure a management slot, and all of the security and
perks that attend thereto. Only now there are not enough slots to
go around. Flattening hierarchy, substituting information systems
for managers, mean the traditional role of the manager—
processing information, channeling information from worker to
senior management and back down again—is no longer needed.

The Baby Boom generation has capably marched through the
workforce. This generation thought it was headed toward a final
decade of maximum personal income prior to retirement. Its
members counted on the rewards due for work well done
throughout the preceding three to four decades. Instead, they find
companies generally under severe financial pressure, willing to
eliminate all but a few of these expensive workers.

Companies are willing to offer employment, but at a reduced
pay scale, and with no promise of advancement. Individuals ask
how the company will value experience, judgment, education,
with limited or no forthcoming answer.

". . . the challenge is not to replace traditional
job security with something closely resembling it.
Rather we must move away (indeed we are moving
away) from a dependent relationship between
employer and employee toward a more collaborative
arrangement."[20]

Flattening organization structures mean less promotion
opportunities. Combined with an excess of candidates, this means

that companies must find an alternative means to reward contributors. 'Progress' must have a new definition.

EXECUTIVE PRESSURES

". . . the most fundamental question a leader can ask is: How likely is it that business can be conducted today the way it was conducted 25, 10, or even five years ago? Is it reasonable to assume that as the world endures an historic cataclysm, that management and leadership can go about taking care of things in the same old way. The answer, plainly, is no.

"A primary lesson of history is that periodically, society needs to make a sharp break with old habits and deliberately learn new ways of behaving. The world is faced with such a moment today."[21]

From the board room to the front line, companies are turning over employees at a great rate. Mergers and redundancy, downsizing and rightsizing, reducing costs to protect margins are all resulting in executive turnover. Individuals who report to the stockholders govern the company. Stockholders, particularly investment groups such as money market and pension funds, want to increase revenues by retaining executives who can expand income to expense ratios.

"While top managers universally recognize their responsibility for developing and allocating a company's scarce assets and resources, their focus on finance and technology often overshadows the task of developing the scarcest resource of all—capable managers."[22]

One has only to look as far as the local newspaper to find evidence of financial pressures facing executives, and consequences for failure.

> "Detroit — General Motors Corp. President Jack Smith, who was chosen to turn the automaker around after a 1992 boardroom coup by outside directors, will become chairman Jan. 1 . . .
>
> "Chairman John Smale, one of the outside directors who led the coup, . . . will move aside to lead a newly formed GM board executive committee.
>
> ". . . The revolt (three years earlier) triggered by billions of dollars in losses . . . forced out Chairman and Chief Executive Robert Stemple.
>
> "Smale became the first GM chairman since the 1950s who was not an executive at the automaker . . .
>
> "GM stock closed at $51.25 yesterday, up $1.87½."[23]

Executives who can meet stockholder objectives are retained. Executives who cannot meet stockholder objectives are let go. Executives are challenged to eliminate expenses and increase profits, or risk losing their positions.

LEADERSHIP MODELS

Many management scenarios are possible, and have been reported on, as executives move into the Information Age. Three possibilities, presented for illustration purposes, are given below. If you work (or worked) in Corporate America, see if you can recognize any of the management styles from your own experience:

Scenario One

They take personal responsibility for moving the company forward. They come to know the business well, and make generally sound judgments. They have a clear vision of where they want the company to go, which they communicate widely. It becomes something of a monopoly game: if they deliver results, they get to pass go, collect $200, and continue to play for Boardwalk. If they cannot deliver results, they step down or move on, clearing the path for subordinates or outsiders, at the board's direction. In the best of circumstances, they have laid a solid foundation for change and then cleared the path for an implementation team to step in.

Scenario Two

They set themselves above the fray, decreeing that change must and will happen. They make 'difficult choices' about eliminating positions, merging businesses. They hand down judgments and mandates, on which subordinates are expected to follow through. They work with trusted associates, people they understand because of shared backgrounds. They move in an insulated world, populated by executives just like themselves, wrestling with similar problems. They know how to keep their own counsel, and create an inner circle of advisors who also know the value of maintaining silence. They are busy and create the appearance of action, which may in fact be more like chaos, all the while hand holding the board and key stockholders. Impatience erupts as they wait for subordinates to deliver results. Needing rapid results and operating at a distance from the business, they can fall prey to subordinates willing to present the appearance of positive outcomes to secure their own positions. One day, the effort implodes and they move on, leaving behind an organization unable to communicate, trust, collaborate or take initiative.

Scenario Three

They join with teams of people, from all levels inside and outside the organization. They facilitate change by being open to contributions of all parties, and by being able to accept different opinions as valuable in their own right. They ask for help. They admit others may have more knowledge than they. They are willing to get their hands dirty, in order to better understand how things work. They inspire confidence by being straight shooters, refusing to modify the truth. They have the trust of their board, because they have never violated that trust. They walk in their employees', customers' and suppliers' shoes. They empower the people around them. Still, they understand it is their responsibility to make and own the toughest decisions, without delay when necessary, without haste when time allows.

Today's literature suggests that the executive of Scenario Three can be a model for success as we move into the Information Age. Scenario Two is the most common approach of a true-blue Industrial Age manager, still trying to maintain control. Scenario One is quite common today, as executives transition from Industrial Age norms of behavior into the freeform environment of the Information Age. However, talking about vision is no longer sufficient, as in Scenario One. Executives must live the business, freely sharing information and power, collaborating without regard to class or race, owning and accepting responsibility of leadership.

> "For decades, we have seen the general manager as chief strategic guru and principal organizational architect. But as the competitive climate grows less stable and predictable, it is harder for one person alone to succeed in that great visionary role. Similarly, as formal, hierarchical structure gives way to networks of personal relationships that work through informal, horizontal communication channels, the image of top

management in an isolated corner office moving boxes and lines on an organization chart becomes increasingly anachronistic."[24]

WHERE DO LEADERS COME FROM?

While leaders are needed throughout the organization, in order to succeed in the Information Age, one can ask how to find those leaders.

"It is significant that very few titles include the word 'leader' and that typically leadership is not discussed extensively in business corporations, even though the very existence of the firm over time requires that leaders be produced from within or brought in from without.[25]

Leaders. Who are they? What are their characteristics? Are leaders born that way, or can they be developed? What can companies do to increase the number of leaders they count within their ranks?

According to Imparato and Harari,

"There are dozens of prescriptions outlining the distinction between a manager's behavior and a leader's behavior. A manager controls, a leader builds commitment; a manager sanctions, a leader inspires; a manager administers, a leader creates; a manager focuses on the routine, a leader focuses on vision."[26]

The qualities of leadership are defined by William Newman, in *'Managers for the Year 2000'*, as:

- 1. *Character* founded on integrity and trust
- 2. *Initiative* which includes risk-taking, self starting, idea generation
- 3. *Desire to serve people*, be a coach, be sufficiently self-confident to be humble, and

> help rather than act as manipulator or
> predator
> - 4. *Intellect*, meaning ability to analyze
>   effectively, learn quickly and have continuing
>   interest in learning
> - 5. *Awareness and perception*, open to what
>   is happening around oneself, and able to
>   evaluate its significance
> - 6. *Foresight/Vision* using intuition and
>   instinct to sense the possibilities, able to look
>   beyond tomorrow and frame decisions within
>   the possibilities of the longer term
> - 7. *Open-mindedness/Flexibility* to consider
>   new facts and ideas, new ways of doing
>   things
> - 8. *Persuasiveness* resulting in the ability to
>   influence others to act, rather than ordering,
>   all-the-while knowing when orders are
>   required, and still able to accomplish the
>   means and ends without appearing to resort
>   to orders.[27]

Leadership is founded on 'people skills', grounded in a realistic assessment of today's workforce and customer needs, and led by a vision of tomorrow's possibilities. Leaders, then, are those who can

- see their decisions from a strategic as well as an operating point of view
- live the business, and be in touch with the people inside and outside the organization who give the company its reason for being
- show the workforce how their contributions are necessary and valued parts of the whole,
- build collaboration and a vision of success among diverse constituencies inside and outside the organization,

- figure needs, process, outcomes, trade-offs, and understand the implications of decisions
- build operating models in which those around them gain as much, or more, than they themselves do.

People can be taught leadership skills. Leaders are not born, they are made. Unfortunately, in Industrial Age companies,

"By the anachronistic structure of our institutions that we so slavishly maintain, and by the incentives we place before people, we are killing off leaders and managers faster than we can possibly develop them. And if we do not stop this, the most heroic measures to prepare people for the unforeseeable conditions of the year 2000 will avail us little."[28]

Changing the way companies operate, as well as the way they motivate and reward people is crucial to the development and retention of leaders. Companies must learn to reward people for collaboration, over competition. Promoting diversity and value-add are at least as, if not more important, than rewarding return on investment and return on sales.

Building the values of the organization into the company's overall system of compensation is one of the fastest means to motivating people at all levels to step beyond managing and acting, to leading—assuming the company's values are leadership driven.

Unfortunately, many companies continue to wrestle with defining their values. Values remain slogans, hashed out in executive roundtables, then printed onto banners and cardboard posters for distribution throughout the organization. Many executives say they believe in the need for values. However, they do not seem to understand that values must come from the heart, and therefore must frame the decisions and actions of the company *all of the time*, not just when it is convenient.

"Few things in life have as much of an impact on people's lives as their jobs. It doesn't matter if you're the head of a giant corporation, or a messenger delivering packages through city streets, our jobs are barometers by which we measure our contributions to society and our own self-worth. When values break down in the workplace, the domino effect ripples straight through us and into every aspect of society. We feel abused and cheated. Our own sense of self-worth and value plummets.

". . . Values transcend business. They are first and foremost about people.

". . . it's becoming increasingly obvious that our current method of downsizing problems away isn't working. Restructuring does nothing for those who lose their jobs, and only creates greater anxiety for those who stay. It doesn't create better service, and it's certainly not doing much for productivity.

". . . Values and business performance go hand in hand. Without one we can't have the other. . . . Business leaders are coming to the conclusion that shareholder wealth cannot be a basis for a company's existence.

". . . When you base your business on a values-based strategy, you're telling the world that you're in it for the long run."[29]

Values must apply to every person, at every level, not just to 'those people out there'. Values must be ingrained into the heart and soul of the company. Managers, especially senior management, must be willing to honor those values in every decision, throughout the organization.

Values and leadership qualities do not magically appear. Leaders can be built and values can be taught. Companies must build leaders at all levels of the company, and teach people to use values in all their decisions. One of the most serious issues facing managers at all levels, then, is getting everyone in the company focused on values and leadership. Developing a competent, committed workforce, able to respond to today's issues and ready to move on to tomorrow's adventures is a major challenge as well as an opportunity.

ROLE OF TRAINING AND CAREER DEVELOPMENT

We talked to many companies, some that recognize people as assets, and some that confessed they do not prize the value of people, but view them as replaceable commodities. Some companies talked about how they struggle to become better at interacting with individuals and groups.

Some companies mentioned that in the late 1960s and early 1970s a hot topic of discussion was the value of individuals and their relationship to the company. They often attributed this topic to the general climate of the time, as the 'flower children' tried to awaken in their elders an awareness and practice of holistic human relations. Then came the 'go-go 80s' when the economy expanded quickly. Many individuals we interviewed said they saw their companies rapidly deploy career development programs in this period. They qualified this observation by saying that, in retrospect, companies probably started the programs because they were 'nice to do.' Companies built the programs because they had extra funds and because excess staff was available to work on such 'niceties.'

At the end of the economic boom of the 1980s, as we experienced a crash on Wall Street and a severe economic downturn, many career development programs were killed. According to those we interviewed, programs were canceled for a number of reasons.

- Companies encountered deep, unpredicted, financial difficulties. They made substantial program cuts throughout, to return to profitability. Development programs were caught in the cuts.

- Companies did not know why they were
  doing the training and development
  programs, or what benefits were being
  derived.
- Training and development programs existed
  as stand alone entities, usually in human
  resources, not part of the business units to
  which they contributed. Therefore, programs
  were easily identified on separate budgets
  and became targets as widespread cost
  cutting efforts took over.
- Companies moved into short-term planning
  modes, unable or unwilling to think past
  surviving the next year or two. They viewed
  development programs as long term
  investments, with limited short term payback
  potential.
- Financial managers increased their power.
  Companies focused on balance sheets in
  response to financial difficulties. Managers
  prized hard capital assets—things which they
  could leverage, borrow on, or otherwise
  value with the bankers. Valuing training and
  development efforts as tangibly as plant and
  equipment seemed impossible; return on
  investment was too nebulous.

Evidence shows that leadership companies are again
investing in training and career development, with notable
changes from the programs of the 1980s. Today, programs are
sponsored and paid for by the business units they are designed to
impact.

Embedding training and career planning in the
business unit makes it much more difficult to
identify it as a separate line item, making it less

> vulnerable to widespread cost cutting during
> economic downturns[30]

commented one human resource manager in a leading financial
institution.

As employees move from one project to another, education
plays a much greater role. Required to take on shorter job
assignments, learn new tasks, build teamwork and facilitation
skills, employees are likely to need much more continuous
education.

> "In Hewlett-Packard's competitive, high-tech
> market, this environment of continual learning is
> integral to work, not just some nice platitude, Davis
> (Claudia Davis, director of education at Hewlett-
> Packard in Palo Alto, Ca.) says. The skills of some
> H-P engineers have a half-life of only 18 months,
> meaning that half of their knowledge becomes
> obsolete in the space of less than two years."[31]

Contracts between individuals and companies are likely to
include rewards for increasing knowledge. They need to
accommodate learning, as individuals prepare to move along,
whether vertically, horizontally, or into another area altogether.

One manager described accountability for managing
diversity and the development process in her company:

> Making line managers responsible for building
> their own replacements, two to three levels down,
> introduces an interesting process. Now part of a
> manager's success depends upon development
> actions of his or her staff. You would be surprised
> how quickly managers become involved in
> identifying and supporting development plans.[32]

What is the penalty for not developing plans with
subordinates, and for not building their own replacements?

First, they don't go anywhere. Next, they get
help changing behavior. Finally, they get help out
the door, because this (developing qualified
successors) is just one of the basics of good
managers. Ultimately, noncompliance is bad for
business.[33]

What if the manager is otherwise a top performer and
producer. Is he still out the door for not developing subordinates?

That is when we and all of our people get to
find out if we are willing to walk the talk.[34]

This manager also talked about the overall role of training
and development in a company.

Training and career development must play two
roles today. First, they must be tools to help
individuals enhance and build additional marketable
skills, in order to maintain their livelihood in a
changing work environment. Second, they must in
some way help people to move on to a new employer
at some time in the future. Since few employees
today can expect lifetime employment in one
company, this seems basic.[35]

In the chapter on Company Success, we provide examples of
companies which understand that employees are not likely to
remain on their payroll forever. We show how these companies go
about supporting that understanding. Remember. Employees
today are likely to have eight different jobs during their work life.
In all likelihood, seven of those will be with some other company.
Working collaboratively on planning for the future can help a
company to achieve maximum productivity and commitment from
workers while they are on board, with limited downside when they
leave.

UNIONS AND TRAINING

> "The traditional labor-management belief that
> the two are opponents, with each trying to get more
> from the other, has built companies where distrust
> and manipulation are so endemic that neither group
> believes in nor cares about the needs of the other. . . .
> Indeed, the new labor-management contract is one of
> partners bent on improving the system, whether
> through employee participation programs or
> increased teamwork."[36]

Pressure is widespread to constrain salaries and traditional benefits such as health care and retirement benefits. Unions are especially sensitive to this issue, as one of their primary benefits to members historically has been increases in wages and benefits. To continue to justify value to their membership, many unions are turning to alternative negotiations such as career development and skill training programs.

When AT&T underwent downsizing efforts in the mid to late 1980s, negotiations with the Communication Workers union included support for retraining efforts, to help individuals identify and prepare for alternative jobs and careers. Such programs have now become standard fare for layoffs and downsizings through 'Ma Bell' and 'Baby Bell' companies.

> "During a recent economic slow-down,
> NUMMI (New United Motor Manufacturing Inc.,
> the auto plant that is a partnership between United
> Auto Workers, General Motors and Toyota) invested
> in training rather than lay-offs. When sales bounced
> back, productivity and quality were even higher than
> before . . ."[37]

REENGINEERING, DOWNSIZING AND OPEN COMMUNICATION

Companies facing downsizing efforts have difficult choices facing them. When facing the decision of whether they should tell employees of impending layoffs, an 'us versus them' mentality can all to easily take hold. 'Us' are the planners of downsizing efforts, the ones who usually expect to stay. 'Them' becomes everyone else, and often, by definition, those most likely to be candidates for downsizing.

Conventional wisdom has taken the position:
- If they tell employees that shortly the company will not need their skills, won't employees depart prematurely?
- Until it is known who is likely to go, why raise alarms with the workforce in general?

Unfortunately, today information moves at lightening speed. Negative news travels as fast as positive news—with greater impact, since the news media has trained us to pay attention when the news is bad.

In the face of downsizing, fear leads people to give negative news greater perceived importance. Imagining the worst, small problems take on big implications. Old tendencies to 'bury the numbers' when they are bad, and to 'wait for things to get better,' become recipes for disaster. Leaders in the Information Age will know that sharing information, good or bad, will lead to opportunities to buy into shared solutions.

In *Rethinking the Corporation*, Tomasko talks about General Motors and Northern Telecom experience with non-traditional plant closings, in which
". . . they gave many more months' notice that
the plants would be shut down than is commonly

provided or legally required. Both companies found that during the period from when the notice was provided to the actual closing, the plants' *productivity soared!* Absenteeism and scrap rate dropped, and product quality and morale were frequently the best ever.

"Why these counterintuitive results? . . . Knowing when 'the assignment' had to end provided a strong focus for everybody's attention and efforts. Knowing the length of the game seemed to motivate the players to give it their best."[38]

Game theory shows that wide distribution of information to all players changes the process of negotiation from antagonism and distrust to mutual goal setting and collaboration. Players share problems and seek mutually beneficial outcomes. In impending downsizings, companies are well advised to openly share the problem with all workers, especially those most likely to be affected, and to include those people in developing potential solutions.

LOOKING AHEAD

"History has shown us several periods characterized by sharp breaks with the past and entirely new sets of realities and demands. . . . we are in the midst of such a period today . . . Epochal transitions show discontinuity with the past . . . historical breaks require a dramatic shift in the very premises of how organizations are managed. Leaders today are challenged to deal with new realities in ways that are radically and qualitatively different from anything they have known. They are asked to 'jump the curve.'

"Jumping the curve means leaving one stage of development for another, leaving one pattern of behavior for another. . . . those who do jump will

find that the next curve does not even exist yet . . . it
is being created by the leaders who are in the very
process of guiding their organizations through
'midair'—the gap between the requirements of
today's fading epoch and the demands of the new era
that is still unsettled and in evolution.

". . . Jumping the curve first requires
organizations to shift their priorities from stabilizing
to innovating . . . The emphasis in the new work
environment is on information and knowledge."[39]

Members of the workforce have asked key questions about
Corporate America, and as a result are now building distance
from the traditional workplace.

- Has the pressure cooker become too highly
  pressurized?
- Are the fears of failure overcoming the
  celebrated wins?
- Are expectations so varied, so large, or so
  unclearly defined as to make it nearly
  impossible to achieve tangible success?

Companies which can resolve the problems to which these
questions allude, will have greater opportunities to attract and
retain the best and the brightest of the workforce in the future.
The very best of the workforce, however, is likely to strike out on
its own, to gain greater control over these key issues.

One major shift of the Information Age is to an
entrepreneurial workforce. The leaders, the success profiles,
already exist: In 1991,

- 12.1 million people ran full-time businesses
  from their homes,
- 11.7 million ran part time businesses, and
- 6.6 million people telecommuted.[40]

"It is no secret that many Fortune 500
companies have lost their luster as places to work. In

a recent study of career preferences conducted by Opinion Research Corp., just 1% of 1,000 adult respondents said they would freely choose to be corporate managers . . .

"The 1993 class at the Harvard business school ranked salary seventh among the reasons for the career choices they made. Leading the list: job content and level of responsibility. Company culture and the caliber of colleagues were close behind."[41]

The challenges and problems discussed in this chapter are only some of the issues facing Corporate America today. As we transition into the Information Age these challenges affect nearly every facet of the way we go to work. Warning signs, examples of successful company experiences and individual initiatives, and issues surrounding diversity, all part of the challenges, are all presented in the following chapters.

IV.
Diversity

Different values and judgments are placed on behaviors based upon race, gender and background. Companies say they will reward one type of behavior, then actually tolerate or even promote another type. Companies also tolerate or reward behavior among one class of people, only to label that same behavior inappropriate for another.

Roosevelt Thomas relates the comments of a white middle manager, who, when asked how promotions are handled, described the company's values.

> "leadership capability, bottom-line results, the ability to work with people, and compassion. . . . That's what they say. But down the hall there's a guy we call Captain Kickass. He's ruthless, mean-spirited, and he steps on people. That's the behavior they really value. Forget what they say."

Not only is this dichotomy hypocritical, it presents a barrier to women and minorities, in that behaving like Captain Kickass is considered inappropriate when coming from a minority.[1]

Our public stereotypes of successful role models vary greatly by sex and race. Think of the number of times you have seen a mainstream movie present a Black, Hispanic or Asian executive or entrepreneur in a main role, as a positive role model. When did you last see a movie with a member of a minority group playing the role of President, when it was not a caricature.

> "Name all the movies you can think of in which a major character is an ambitious career woman who has risen high in her field. And now: In how many of those movies is this character a likable, sympathetic, warm, and loving person?"[2]

SOME FACTS ON DIVERSITY

Diversity in the workforce is a given in the United States today. The workforce will become even more diverse in the future. Learning to respect and work with diversity has already become a success factor for companies moving into the Information Age.

Diverse Workforce

Inequities exist in how various constituencies are treated in the workplace. Barriers to entry and to advancement for any individual will inhibit our competitive position in the global marketplace and in the Information Age. First, some statistics to frame the argument for change.

> "In today's brain-based global economy, the ability to attract and retain talented people becomes the most important competitive edge a company can have. . . . Demographic data suggest that only 15 percent of the net additions to the American work force between 1993 and the year 2000 will be native-born white males. Therefore it seems obvious that . .
> management should waste no time in actively pursuing top talent from among women, minorities, and immigrants."[3]

> ". . . more than half the U.S. work force now consists of minorities, immigrants, and women, so white, native-born males, though undoubtedly still dominant, are themselves a statistical minority.[4]

> ". . . nearly all of the growth in the labor force between now and (the year) 2000 will occur in nations with predominately non-Caucasian populations. . . . In the United States, for example, the average white female is 33 years old and has (or

will have) 1.7 children. Corresponding figures for blacks are 28 and 2.4, and for Mexican-Americans, 26 and 2.9."[5]

In 1992, the Glass Ceiling commission, headed by Secretary of Labor Robert Reich, looked at the demographics of the companies on the Fortune 1000 and Fortune 500 Service Company lists. In their Report on Corporate America, they reported that white males made up:

- 43% of the total labor force
- 97% of senior level decision-making managers

Of the 3% of senior level managers who were non-white male:

- 0.6% were black,
- 0.4% were Latino
- 0.3% were Asian, and
- 1.7% were Other

The commission also reported that:

- Black males with professional degrees earn 79¢ for every $1 earned by white males with the same credentials,
- Black females earn 60¢ for every $1 earned by white males.[6]

Inequities do exist. The question is who will accept responsibility for implementing change.

Black Owned Companies

Like other minorities, business owners who happen to be Black have become forces in their respective markets.

The Black Enterprise 100s are industrial and service companies in business for over one year, that are at least 51% black-owned. In 1994, the BE 100s employed almost 48,000 people, and the largest companies on the list posted sales of $6.7 billion in 1994, a 9.27% increase over 1993. Categories leading the list in terms of sales included auto dealerships, food service, media and technology—a diverse set of industries.[7]

These companies represent opportunities for employment. They buy products and services from other companies, which result in job and revenue opportunities for more people and businesses. And they have amassed enough capital and management strength to now focus on politics.

Similar growth in influence is occurring in other ethnically based segments of the population, including Asian and Hispanic communities.

> "Since 1965 a fifth migration wave has once again transformed the landscape of the United States, turning it more than ever into a multiracial society, swelling the work force, and creating a new set of social tensions. In 1990 the flow of legal immigrants reached more than 1.5 million, a number about equal to that of Ellis Island's peak year. Millions more entered the United States illegally in the 1980s, most of them crossing the largely unpoliced 2,000-mile border with Mexico. How many millions no one really knows . . .
>
> "Before 1965 the majority of immigrants were still overwhelmingly European, and in the early post-World War II years they were largely middle class. . . . But by the 1980s immigrants from Asia, Latin America, and the Caribbean accounted for 83 percent of the new influx. While large numbers came to escape the wars and repression in such places as El Salvador, Guatemala, Ethiopia, Cuba, and Vietnam, the primary motive for most, as in the great migrations of the nineteenth century, was to earn a living."[8]

Women

While not a minority, women have become a major constituency in the workplace.

> "The most notable alteration in labor force composition has been the postwar influx of women into the job market, particularly married women with children. In 1978, 41 percent of the workforce consisted of women, nearly half of them less than thirty-five years of age, about one-fourth between sixteen and twenty-four, one in six a college graduate, and over 70 percent high school graduates.[9]

In a survey of 300 females entering midlife, 94% of whom were managers and executives,
- 87% had made or were considering major life changes
- 45% had changed jobs, started businesses, or were considering those options[10]

In a 1992 study of 439 executive women, 37% responded that they did not have children, as compared to 5% of executive men in a 1989 study.[11]

Women are leaving Corporate America, and they are doing so at a higher percentage rate than their male counterparts. In a 1993 survey of people who received MBAs over the previous 10 years from Stanford University, only 8% of the men had left large corporations to start their own businesses, while 22% of women, *nearly three times as many*, had left to do so.[12]

These few statistics point to a very different viewpoint for about half of the workforce. The differences in view affect choices about contribution and commitment, as we will see later on.

Reverse Discrimination

While it is customary to talk about the need to address racial and gender inequities, concern also exists about reverse discrimination. White males are heard to comment that women and minorities are taking jobs away from them. Although this may be the case from time to time, the volume of court cases does not support the contention that this is a major factor in the workplace. The Bureau of National Affairs, in their Employment Discrimination Report, reported that from 1990 to 1994 there were:

- 3,000 discrimination opinions in the courts, and of those 3,000 discrimination opinions, there were:
- 100 reverse discrimination cases, and there were
- 6 cases where reverse discrimination was legally established[13]

As Frank McCoy pointed out in his article, while there are general assumptions that minorities are taking jobs away from otherwise qualified white males, the reverse discrimination suits represent only 3.3% of all discrimination cases over four years. Reverse discrimination suits were upheld by the courts in only 0.2% of the total cases brought between 1990 and 1994.

EDUCATION STATISTICS

According to American business historian Stuart Bruchey,
"The United States has more functional illiterates than any other industrial country. A twelve-nation study of seven subjects, including math, science, reading comprehension, and literature, found the national average comprehensive scores of Americans ranking in the lower third.

American students were poorer in math than those of any other nation tested."[14]

In 1991, of all the college degrees conferred,
- 83.6% of Bachelor's Degrees went to whites, and
- only 16.4% went to blacks, Hispanics and other minorities.

In 1976, fall enrollment in colleges was split at
- 84.3% white, and
- 15.7% minority, including 9.6% Black.

In the fall of 1992,
- white enrollment as a percent of the whole fell to 77.5%, while
- minority enrollment had increased to 22.5%, Black enrollment held steady at 9.9%.[15]

As a result of these statistical indicators, it is expected that blacks, Hispanics and other minorities in the future will walk away with a greater share of Bachelor Degrees, potentially opening more doors for participation in entry level management and other white collar positions.

Meanwhile, only 77.7% of Masters Degrees and 65.7% of Doctoral Degrees went to whites, a significant fall off in emphasis on post four-year education as compared to undergraduate studies. Minorities, in many cases assumedly pursuing credentials to level the playing field, were awarded 22.3% of all Master's Degrees and 34.3% of all doctoral degrees.[16]

MINORITY BUSINESSES

Minority businesses are becoming a factor, in the economy, in politics, as competitors, as business partners. In some ways, minority businesses are ideally positioned to capitalize on opportunities of the Information Age.

Minority businesses are often small and flexible, run by owners who are passionate about what they are doing. Owners are usually risk takers and, to the extent that they are experiencing success in their business, they are being rewarded and reinforced for taking risks. Their workers are people who have experienced little or no security working for large companies in Corporate America. Previous experience with discrimination in Corporate America increases identity with and commitment to working in minority owned and managed businesses.

Minority business owners and leaders network. They join community and social organizations to further their business goals. They are often committed to giving back, which means offering time and effort in a variety of areas, inside and outside of the business. Social contribution efforts give them exposure and put them close to consumers. Networking exposes minorities to conversations and insights that can lead to better understanding of emerging critical needs, around which to build new product and service offerings.

MINORITIES AND POLITICS

As more minority businesses succeed, their influence on politics and economics will increase. It is like looking at the product life cycle of any business. In the beginning, there is slow, sometimes painfully slow, growth over a long period, followed by rapid and dramatic increases in income, size and influence as the product (or, in this case, the business sector) takes off.

Approaches to political influence are changing.

"The threat to eliminate minority set-asides and other provisions designed to ensure that black-owned businesses participate in the business of the nations . . . is serious enough to prompt several of the CEOs of these businesses (the largest black industrial/service companies) to organize with the intent of establishing a political action committee to advance the black business agenda."[17]

It can be expected that minorities and women will increase their influence in politics over time.

FRANCHISING

Both women and minorities are using franchises as vehicles to open and build businesses, using the structure and support of the franchiser to facilitate success in their venture. Some believe that franchise businesses, having the characteristics of 'small business' better fits the needs of their local communities. At the same time, the backing of a franchise, and the due diligence process at point of entry, contribute to higher success rates for these small businesses, as compared to stand alone start-ups.

Franchise Industry Statistics:

- 3,500 franchise companies,
- with 550,000 outlets,
- in 65 different industries,
- employing 8 million people,
- using suppliers who employ 2.4 million additional people,
- had sales increases of 460% over the past two decades,
- with 1994 industry sales reaching an estimated $970 billion,
- and sales for 1995 projected to increase 15% over 1994.[18]

Black Enterprise Magazine suggests that minorities look at several criteria when selecting a franchise relationship, and to that end has published a list, "BE's 20 best franchise opportunities". The characteristics they recommend a potential franchisee look for, include:

- advertising in the black press
- programs and policies aimed at minority recruitment
- record keeping on minority involvement in franchises
- availability of financial assistance programs
- ongoing marketing and advertising support
- independent franchise association within the industry.[19]

"After more than a decade of rhetoric about diversity initiatives, franchisors are still, 'not making any great effort to recruit or retain minority entrepreneurs,' says Susan P. Kezios, president of the Chicago-based American Franchisee Association and Women in Franchising, a franchisee advocacy group. 'There is a perception out there on the part of franchisors that minorities don't have any money, so why should they waste their time recruiting them.'

"More disturbing, a number of franchisors are willing to rectify the situation only when faced with discrimination suits."[20]

Franchising companies would be well advised to evaluate their accomplishments in attracting and recruiting franchisees outside of the white male population. They need to look at their own internal biases, as well as their training, community outreach, financing and supplier programs. Franchising organizations would do well to understand a major source of growth in the Information Age is likely to come from female and minority constituents, who are going to do business with those they most respect and those with whom they most identify. If franchising organizations are not aggressively moving to capture marketshare with these two growth segments of the entrepreneurial workforce, they would be well advised to ask themselves why.

FINANCING

One traditional barrier to development in minority and low income neighborhoods has been the difficulty of attracting financing. Banks have historically had no roots in these communities, and bankers have no personal relationships there. Lending funds ultimately comes down to the confidence of the lending institution in the target business, the market and the owner.

> "As minorities continue to fight for a bigger share of the $970 billion franchise industry, a new battle plan calls for greater community involvement. Some financial institutions, such as Bankers Trust in New York, are already teaming up with community development corporations to bring more franchise outlets to urban areas and recruit minorities to run them."[21]

Without relationships in the community, banks lack a fundamental base on which to assess the potential viability of the business owner and plan. The trust factor, that unspoken variable in lending, cannot come into play, because there is no basis for a relationship, let alone trust. And so lending institutions tend to miss out on participation in significant portions of the economy—minority neighborhoods and minority owned businesses.

One initiative in New York is designed to address this problem of lack of relationship between banks and the local community, its leaders and potential business owners. This initiative brings together three entities, a bank, an umbrella development organization, and local community leadership. This initiative is based upon the concept that local organizations best know the market and the people within the market, and that while banks may not know the people or understand the community, they can work through outreach organizations to invest in the most likely success candidates

Local Initiatives Support Corp. (LISC), the umbrella group, is a non-profit organization. In conjunction with the bank, Bankers Trust, LISC has funded a $3.5 million project to support franchise development in minority communities and with minority ownership. Community Development Corporations (CDCs) are non profit organizations controlled by local residents and business people. CDCs are believed to have the best relationships with, and working knowledge of, people in the local community. CDCs, therefore are in a position to supply lending institutions with assistance in assessing viability of various potential business owners and business plans.

In this three way project, while Bankers Trust and LISC are funding the project, five CDCs support franchise owners by locating low-cost real estate, working to minimize crime, helping to hire employees and implementing marketing efforts. Through the CDC, the bank does become involved in the minority community, and begins to build experience which, it is hoped, will build confidence about the viability of businesses and their owners, and lead to future investments in the community.[22]

STRATEGIC ALLIANCES

Strategic alliances can play a significant role in the evolution of any business. They can be especially valuable to minorities and women, who are seeking to extend their expertise, market reach, experience and resources, while operating small businesses. Strategic alliances with major firms can help small business owners by providing preferred status as vendors or suppliers, leveraging strengths of the individual parties, and making small businesses appear larger, more substantial than they really are. For large business, partnering with small, women or minority owned business can mean access to otherwise limited markets, additional expertise without taking on the expense of additional payroll, and opportunity to experiment (R&D investment is a critical success factor in the Information Age) without losing focus on core business initiatives.

TEAMS AND DIVERSITY

Given the complexity of cultural issues, and the need to integrate diverse backgrounds in order to boost company success, managers will benefit from building social, team oriented skills.

"Data suggest that the fastest growing demographic sectors in the United States are non-English speaking, non-European groups. If an organization wishes to sell products and services to these groups, commonsense management would seek to incorporate the cultural insights of group members into decision making—as employees, subcontractors, joint-venture partners, and consultants.[23]

". . . it now appears that teams indirectly support an important workplace initiative—diversity. When team members are forced to work closely together toward common goals, the most unlikely alliances can, and do, emerge."[24]

The act of forming goals around which the group can converge, leads to focus of the group on task-based, rather than bureaucratic-based activity. While relationships are extremely important in team performance, traditional emphasis on congruence falls away in favor of broad based analysis of problems and potential solutions, focused on delivering a superior outcome.

One major barrier to self managed teams is the traditional approach in American business to management by hierarchy. In addition to the old assumption that someone in power will step in to arbitrate or to rescue, hierarchy implies a code of behavior. Hierarchy assumes there is a boss in the relationship—and by definition there can only be one.

> "If you begin with these assumptions (hierarchy=boss=only one), then . . . refusal to take the subordinate role means, ipso facto, that (he)/she wants to be the dominant one."[25]

In teams there are no dominants or subordinates, no boss, no hierarchy. There are only equals, all with different skills and backgrounds, working together to get a job done.

Confusion may erupt among team members as people from different backgrounds are likely to react differently. One team member may fight, or express opposition, simply for the purpose of staking out territory, or establishing connection. Another team member may have a highly collaborative background, having been trained to avoid confrontation and facilitate congruence. Putting these two together could result in seriously mixed, and untrue messages.

The first team member assumes he has overpowered the other without any opposition, labels the other a wimp, and loses respect for the other's potential contribution. The second team member identifies the first as combative, uncooperative, unable to contribute to a group process, and withdraws from interaction. In fact, both team members were simply using unspoken, but misunderstood, language to get to know each other.

The unfortunate part is that they are both likely to require significant time to pass, along with intervention and coaching, in order to get past the stereotypes they both presented, and their impressions of each other.

Cooperation and communication are crucial to team success. Congruence is not. Respect for variety and flexibility in accepting others' solutions, and willingness to set aside personal agenda in favor of team are all important. In self directed work teams,

> "Team members have to come to grips with each other and their differences face-to-face, day to day, in order to get their jobs done."[26]

Failure to do so results in failure of the team, which by definition, means failure for the individual participants, who depend upon successful outcomes of the team in order to obtain income and future employment opportunities.

That is not to say that teams form easily, or become functional overnight. Forming, storming, norming and performing are standard phases in team formation. In the case of self directed work teams, the team has nowhere to go but inside the group to work through the issues that attend each of the four phases.

WHY DO PEOPLE MOVE ON?

Why are women and minorities leaving large companies? Reasons cited are that they are not fulfilled, they are bored, they are away from home too much, and they are fed up with the bureaucracy.

We believe the following comments apply to minorities as well as women. Betsy Morris brought together a group of women whom she described as follows.

> "They are serious career women. They are trailblazers. They think lateral moves are for losers. But increasingly they have become unhappy with their lives, and some of them have made big changes."[27]

> "It is clearly a time of reckoning for baby-boomer businesswomen—the first big generation of 'skirts,' . . . to hit the age of 40 in a business suit. In

many cases, the soul-searching has little, directly, to
do with frustration about the glass ceiling. . . (or)
from so-called work-family struggles.

". . . In great numbers, women executives
emerge from this period making decisive midcourse
corrections. Many have simply wearied of the male-
dominated game and seek to do business more on
their own terms. They change not only their jobs but
their ideas of success as well."[28]

We made similar observations as a result of our research—
that women exhibit a need to find or create a work environment
where the rules are different, where they can more closely identify
with the role models. In one instance, we talked about turnover
and mentoring with an executive in a major consulting firm
headquartered in the East. This person observed that while it is
possible to attract women and minorities in early stages of their
careers, it is much more difficult to retain them into late stages,
when they conceivably would join senior management ranks.

We actively recruit women and minorities. We
are more successful attracting women than
minorities. Part of this is the high demand for
college educated minorities—they have so many
choices, and we are only willing to go so far in the
bidding war to attract them to our company.

Once on board, we assign these people to a
mentor, who is supposed to coach the person,
provide insight and inside information, and
generally look out for and encourage the person's
success. The mentors are part of the firm's senior
management team and therefore are assumed to have
the clout to look out for their candidates, and to be
able to advocate on their behalf.

Now, you need to understand the nature of our
organization. We do not expect to provide lifetime
employment to any but a few of our firm members—

and I believe we are pretty clear about that in our hiring process.

We expect to provide training, interesting projects, and exposure to a variety of companies who are our clients. After a number of years, most of our employees move on, usually to client firms, which is good for us. We assume that if someone worked here, and had a good experience, and leaves respecting the firm, they will remember that when it comes time to hire a consulting firm. So, if we are able to move people into the corporate market, and if they believe in the quality of the work they were doing here and the caliber of people they worked with here, we think that is going generate new business for us in the future.[29]

We will come back to this firm's approach to assessing reputation among exiting employees in the chapter on Company Success. In the meanwhile, let's focus on this firm's record of retaining and promoting women and minorities.

We are having a hard time hanging onto them. Just about the time they become really valuable to us, they are very attractive to the marketplace as well. They get very good offers from other companies. Maybe they get an offer for a position which would be equal to a promotion here in this company. And maybe they are not considered eligible for that promotion for another year or two—or we just do not have a slot available. So, they move on.[30]

What about the mentors. Can't they influence these people to stay?

Some mentors are better than others. Some seem to keep their candidates here longer, when it is appropriate. But when someone comes in with a great job offer, what are you going to say? Don't do it for the good of the firm?[31]

We asked one final question. Did this executive really believe women and minorities would leave if they felt totally identified with the firm—if there were a number of minorities on the Executive Committee, if the senior management of the firm was also part of their inner circle of friends, if their needs beyond compensation were being met, if they knew they were going to make it to the top management ranks within a defined timeframe? Our interviewee answered:

> I don't know, because that's not the case.[32]

SPIRALING AND THE GLASS CEILING

The issue of turnover among women and minorities, moving from one good offer to the next, was discussed by an executive in charge of compensation for a major food company in the Midwest. He called it spiraling. He felt spiraling has serious negative implications for breaking through the glass ceiling. These are his observations.

> I am a dinosaur, you know. I have worked for this firm all of my career. And with only a few years to go before retirement, I will probably stay to the end. Now you, on the other hand, you have had three employers in the 10 years I have known you. You have successfully leaped from one company to another, building income, title and perks along the way. In fact, I am willing to bet you make more than I do today, at least in direct salary. But I stay for other things, such as the stock equity I have built thanks to the performance of this company, the investment I have in various projects throughout the company, the friendships I have built here, and so on. What you have done is what I call the upward spiral of diversity hiring. It seems to happen to women and minorities all the time, and I personally

believe it is a major contributor to what you call the glass ceiling effect.

Let me explain. Each time you get to a certain level and responsibility in your career, you become attractive to the marketplace. You also do a good job of joining industry organizations, so that people outside of the company are aware of your existence and accomplishments. Then something in your current company begins to annoy you—you don't get along with your boss, you don't like the projects to which you are assigned, a project fails, you don't like the travel. Whatever. When the annoyance gets bad enough, you spiral out, pursuing one of those offers from some other company.

Now you are hitting a glass ceiling, as you try to crack senior management ranks and become a member of the inner circle. Unfortunately as long as you keep spiraling out, you will probably not become a member of the senior management team. Teams take awhile to form, and even longer to become fully functional. Senior management teams face a lot of stress, and they want to know that potential members have the staying power to hang around when times get bad.

Your career and mine have taken very different paths. I have stayed here through good times and bad. I have learned a different set of skills to get me through the down cycles—things like building support networks, learning patience, developing a sense of continuity, which really means being around long enough to see projects that I believed in come back to life after being initially turned down. You, on the other hand, have skipped from one success plateau to the next. You have yet to build the skills of 'survival' in the down cycles. You get impatient. Those are not bad things. But they mean you look at the world differently, you approach change differently, and you send different signals to your

employer. These signals, mind you, may indicate to
them that you are not ready to be trusted with the
keys to the executive washroom. They are going to
watch you. They want to see if you will learn to stick
around, if you can build support networks, if you can
survive failures as well as you celebrate your
successes.

Of course, you don't have to stay. There are
plenty of employers looking for good minorities and
women. But its like constantly running sprints. At
each new company, you come in like a house afire,
with something to prove. Each time you move, you
have to build a successful track record, and do it
relatively quickly, in order to live up to their
expectations. That can begin to tire you out after
awhile, and then what are you going to do? Do you
want to keep having to prove yourself to the next
employer?[33]

Sticking it out through tough times was discussed by Patricia
Sellers in an article on executives who 'bounced back' from
failure. Sellers described the situation of a woman who was the
highest-ranking female line manager at a major financial
institution.

After a business failure, for which this woman 'was held
accountable, but not responsible', she was removed from her job
and thought about leaving the company. Instead, she chose to
stay, and take on a new, albeit less prestigious assignment. Says
her manager today, she is

"an example of someone whose career was
stalled but who had the courage to take on an
incredibly difficult challenge. Too many people in
corporate life look for the safe place, and as a result
stay stuck in a band."[34]

Since this failure a few years ago, this manager has sought
the assistance of her management, learned from her failure, and
since been promoted for her later success. She could have easily

spiraled out of the company, and admits that she considered that option. However, staying through the aftermath of the crisis, with a supportive company, who knew about and valued her previous successes, has resulted in, among other things, crashing through the glass ceiling into the senior management ranks of a major financial institution.[35]

DISCRIMINATION COMES IN ALL KINDS OF FORMS

Differences in upbringing and acculturation result in different interpretations of behavior. A female lawyer for a west coast law firm experienced conflicts in norms of behavior.

"There was a code of behavior, and she always felt she was bumping up against it. 'The times I got the biggest pats on the back were the times I screamed the loudest,' she recalls." [36]

The lawyer expressed frustration over having to participate in a meeting of 6 lawyers, lasting 2 hours, arguing over a $7,000 issue.

"They were staking out their territory, a colleague explained. 'You had to play the game that way. If you didn't, it was perceived as weakness.
'It wasn't that their way is bad', she says, 'It's just that it isn't my way.' She realized how far she was drifting from her idealistic goals . . . (and ultimately left the firm) . . .
(Some women find) the chase just gets ludicrous, especially when it leads up a male-style hierarchy they don't necessarily believe in, and further and further away from what they love best to do."[37]

Born To Behave

> "At work, women often take it personally when
> someone disagrees with them or openly argues . . ."[38]

While disagreement, among men, often is a basis for being taken seriously.

> "It is frequently observed that male speakers
> are more likely to be confrontational by arguing,
> issuing commands, and taking opposing stands for
> the sake of argument, whereas females are more
> likely to avoid confrontation by agreeing, supporting,
> and making suggestions rather than commands."[39]

It is also important to understand gender based behavior, to better understand both the way one person is likely to act, and the way another is likely to react.

> "Walter Ong argues that 'adversativeness'—a
> tendency to fight—is universal, but 'conspicuous or
> expressed adversativeness is a larger element in the
> lives of males than of females.' In other words,
> females may well fight, but males are more likely to
> fight often, openly, and for the fun of it.
> ". . . A modern day equivalent of the bonding
> that results from ritual opposition can be found in
> business, where individuals may compete, argue, or
> even fight for their view without feeling personal
> enmity."[40]

Aggression

Aggression is one behavior about which genders are taught very different rules. Boys are generally taught that aggression is appropriate, it enhances their 'manhood.' On the other hand,

> "From childhood, girls learn to temper what
> they say so as not to sound too aggressive—which
> means too certain."[41]

> "Both women and men pay a price if they do not behave in ways expected of their gender: Men who are not very aggressive are called 'wimps,' whereas women who are not very aggressive are called 'feminine.' Men who are aggressive are called 'go-getters,' though if they go too far, from the point of view of the viewer, they may be called 'arrogant.' This can hurt them, but not nearly as much as the innumerable labels for women who are thought to be too aggressive—starting with the most hurtful one: bitch."[42]

Crying

Another major behavior that results in gender-based interpretation is crying. In today's corporate world, crying is considered a sign of weakness. The crier can be penalized for exhibiting this behavior, up to and including denial of promotion opportunity and limiting of access to the inner circle.

> "Says Kristin Snowden, a second-year University of Chicago student who worked for several years as a Price Waterhouse auditor: 'There is a way people are supposed to behave at work at large companies, and it's based on a male model that is hundreds of years old. Women cry more often than men, for example: we find that it is an effective way to relieve stress. But you are never, ever supposed to cry on the job if you work at a large company'."[43]

Generally, boys have been taught that crying is a form of weakness. They are rebuked for the behavior. They receive little comfort until they stop crying. They learn to go to great lengths to avoid any public expression that even comes close to crying, up to and including denying feelings and running away.

Girls, on the other hand, learn that it is okay to express through crying, even in public, as long as the display does not go on for too long and is not too loud. Girls, are comforted by others when they express feelings through crying. Little wonder women are seen to cry at work, while among men, crying is a rare sight indeed.

> "Tears are the river of life, shed in joy as well
> as in sadness and fear."[44]

Make no mistake, however. In business, as well as politics, both men and women are usually severely penalized for crying. Ed Muskie's presidential campaign fell apart after he cried during a meeting with the press in New Hampshire. Pat Schroeder, with tears, announced she would not pursue her political dreams. She was then labeled as a weak female by some of the press and certain political commentators.

RECOMMENDATIONS

According to the statistics above, we already have a diverse workforce. Many of our largest companies are headquartered and operate in very diverse markets, such as New York, Detroit, Miami, Southern California. And yet they continue to exhibit shortfalls in promoting minorities into mid and upper management in large numbers.

Senior Management

The highest levels of each company must lead the efforts of building a more diverse, connected workforce, if their companies are to be highly successful. Other success factors of Information Age companies come into play as well when developing a more diverse workforce:
- commitment to change over years rather months;
- accountability at all levels;

- training in new behaviors and skills;
- follow up associated with continuous learning.

Cost of Turnover

Attending to worker concerns can contribute to the profitability of companies, as well as the well being of employees. Just because 9-to-5, 5-day, 40-hour-weeks work well for white males, does not mean they work well for all others. As women and minorities cope with child care, pursuit of education, elderly care, family needs and other priorities outside the workplace, they require flexibility and support from their employers. If they consistently do not receive that support, they are likely to move on once they identify a better opportunity. Cox and Blake estimate the savings in turnover for a 10,000 employee company. They base the estimate on a scenario in which women and racial or ethnic minorities make up 35% of the population. They assume a white male turnover rate of 10%, double that for women and minorities, using previous data on differential turnover rates. They assume that better management practices could halve the turnover. Cox and Blake then estimate the savings resulting from halving turnover among women and minorities, for that 10,000 employee company, to be worth $3.5 million annually.[45]

Market Reputation

A company's ability to attract and retain the best of the workforce can be strongly influenced by market reputation. Articles and books have been written about the best companies for women and minorities. Peers discuss experiences. Magazines publish lists of companies with positive and negative attributes. Associations share information with their constituencies about companies, pro and con. Smart workers look for this kind of information when considering job changes. They factor into salary negotiations the support they expect to receive from employers.

One company in the midwest, with a poor reputation for respecting and promoting women and minorities, at one point in time had a 30% workforce shortage in its computer programming department. Computer programming was critical to the success of the company's operations. At the same time, peer companies in the same community were at full staff in their computer programming departments. It was not until the company began offering salaries at 25% above market that the shortfall was corrected.[46]

Management Requirements

When addressing issues of valuing and promoting women and minorities, some companies cited their inability to break a collegial approach of promoting those with whom they are most comfortable—socially, emotionally and professionally.

Breaking through this barrier requires commitment to measurement of management performance in conducting reviews and promotions. It requires absolutely fact based reviews, which emphasize assigned tasks and roles and de-emphasize subjective measures.

> "In a supportive work environment, differences become assets, opportunities for innovation and competitive advantage. For example, by changing perspectives about employee development and coaching, one organization was able to better support its diversity climate.
>
> ". . . Involving managers and employees in the assessment (of diversity within the organization) will increase their level of commitment to working toward the diversity goals and vision."[47]

Managers must be required to define skill requirements for every job in the organization. Managers need to assess employee performance against tasks specific to the job assignment, sticking to the facts. Managers need to confirm their assessment with one or more second opinions, whether from human resources, higher levels of management and/or peer groups.

Managers need to inform subordinates of any concerns, including the source, so that individuals have an opportunity to take responsibility for addressing the concerns. With information, biases of individual managers may be more easily identified, and then appropriately addressed through their manager and human resource intervention.

Managers must also be sensitive to the role conditioning plays in the way we judge each others' behaviors.

> ". . . a woman is in a double bind. Everything she does to enhance her assertiveness risks undercutting her femininity, in the eyes of others. And everything she does to fit expectations of how a woman should talk risks undercutting the impression of competence that she makes."[48]

It is very easy for one to observe of another, 'So far as I know, he has no biases against women, minorities, etc. . . .' However, evaluation of relevant statistics can be the real indicators. How many women and minorities has the manager hired, promoted, groomed, put onto prominent teams, advocated for or otherwise stood up for, over the course of time. Actions do often speak louder than words, particularly in the case of bias. Senior management would be well advised to be cognizant of the actions they themselves, and their managers, take, and the implications.

CALL TO ACTION

Why should companies care about the relationship between employer and employee? It must be remembered that although there is an excess of employees in the workforce today, thanks to the Baby Boom generation, in another 10 to 20 years, the workforce will shrink and companies will be competing to attract the workers they need.

Diversity Is A Fact

By now it should be clear that diversity is a major factor in the business community and workforce of the United States. We can either ignore the issues that go with diversity, or we can choose to find lasting solutions. There are solid financial and business productivity reasons for tackling diversity issues head on.

> "Diversity is likely to breed tension, conflict, misunderstanding and frustration unless an organization develops a culture that supports, honors and values differences."[49]

A number of companies that we interviewed confessed in private that they did not believe they did a good, or even adequate, job in retaining or promoting minorities, including women. All of the companies we talked with indicated they believed they must one way or another learn to master the issue of fully integrating a diverse workforce. However, with few exceptions, the companies we interviewed lacked solid plans, or a vision, of how they intended to accomplish this.

> ". . . the world you live in is not the one everyone lives in, and the way you assume is *the* way to talk is really only *one* way, quite different from how others might talk in the same situation."[50]

Competitive Advantage

It is possible to build in competitive advantage through diversity. Cox and Blake identify six areas in which diversity efforts will impact the business:
- cost
- resource acquisition
- marketing
- creativity
- problem-solving
- organizational/systems flexibility[51]

Cox and Blake, and others, identify specific costs, or negative impacts which result from failure to build a diverse, connected workforce and environment in each of the six impact areas.

cost - failed or poor efforts at integrating result in increased turnover, loss of output, lower productivity

resource acquisition - ability to attract a premium skilled workforce is a function of access to all workers, not to a limited segment of the population. Limited access to workers increases salary cost and reduces options.

marketing - diversity within organizations leads to cultural sensitivity, which will be an advantage in accessing markets around the globe which do not have a Caucasian heritage. Limited access to markets results in limited opportunities to sell products, and over time causes downward pressure on profits.

creativity - non-conformity and variety will improve creativity, a critical skill when pursuing mass customization. Inability to understand and customize products and services to customer specific needs will lead to uncompetitive market position and loss of marketshare.

problem-solving - diversity of backgrounds and experience will lead to more creative, broad based approaches and higher quality solutions. Improving solutions will increase a company's marketability, profitability, and productivity.

organizational/systems flexibility - diversity will help to break down standardized approaches, leading to more fluid environments. This will lead to greater flexibility, broader perspectives, and an ability to react more quickly, at less cost.[52]

Can Companies Learn?

One question is whether companies will use available research in order to learn and to develop a more capable workforce. The results of studies pointing to the value of heterogeneous work teams were printed between 1965 and 1986—this is not new knowledge.[53]

ONE SUCCESSFUL COMPANY

In the next chapter, you will see cases on companies we interviewed, which illustrate successful employee relations practices. We begin the transition to the next chapter here, with a story about Xerox.

We include Xerox because of their commitment to facing their challenges and effecting change. In the past two decades, Xerox has seen enormous changes, which are best summed up in the book, 'The 100 Best Companies to Work for in America'.

> "Xerox is America's corporate success story of the 1980s. At the beginning of the decade, it looked like a sure loser as its once dominant grip on the photocopying market was rapidly slipping away to Japanese competitors. When we considered Xerox for our list in the early 1980s, we didn't feel it measured up. Employee morale was in the pits; employees talked of the erosion of a humane culture that had been so carefully nurtured by founder Joe Wilson. But we have no reservations about including

Xerox in this edition. The company has undergone a radical transformation that has seen Xerox win back customers from the Japanese through a single-minded focus on quality, while revitalizing the people-oriented values of the Wilson era."[54]

In the 1990s, in the face of downsizings and profitability pressures, Xerox has continued to make progress in building a diverse workforce and a culture of inclusion. One manager at Xerox talked to us about the process of building a diverse workforce, and about what it has taken to come as far as they have.

We held people accountable. We assumed nothing. We told managers we expected them to find, train, groom and promote minorities and women, and then we helped educate them on how to do that. We created urgency at all levels—reporting on what we had achieved from board meetings to department reviews. We explained the need for diversity: that we are a global company, and we must be able to understand and respond to the needs of a diverse consumer. We penalized those who did not get it. Failure to act on diversity meant loss of promotion opportunity, and possibly, ultimately, loss of job with the company. We talked openly with our people about the frustrations. White male managers were encouraged to discuss their responses to working with people unlike themselves. In job interviews, we told potential job candidates that diversity was a core value, and encouraged them to reflect on how that might affect their career here. As we promoted minorities and women, we told them we expected more than job performance from them; we expected them to be role models for and mentors to those who would follow. We encourage support groups, and have seen some of them become incubators for addressing issues of coping and career management, among other things.[55]

Roosevelt Thomas, in an article called, From Affirmative Action to Affirming Diversity, identifies one component of a balanced strategy to make diversity work at Xerox. Roosevelt says the people at Xerox

> ". . . concentrate on managerial training, not so much on managing diversity as on just plain managing people. What the company discovered when it began looking at managerial behavior toward minorities and women was that all too many managers didn't know enough about how to manage anyone, let alone people quite different from themselves."[56]

The above story represents only part of the effort Xerox has put into learning to handle the complex issues surrounding diversity. The people of Xerox have worked hard to create a diverse workforce. Initiatives are driven from the top of the organization, and all levels are held accountable, which is what it takes to effect real change in an organization. For the effort, and even more for the success, congratulations to Xerox.

V.
Company Success

Forward thinking companies and individuals are searching for new ways to interact, to achieve business and personal goals. Emphasis is placed upon independence, personal accountability, trust, collaboration, and continuous learning.

In the past 10 years, we have lived through very difficult times. Company downsizings result in distrust and survivor guilt in employees. Outplaced employees move on to form small businesses and operate as independent contractors. Of those who remain working within company structures, attitudes and expectations are changing. All three groups, company, employees and independent workers are looking for ways to increase agility and competitiveness in the marketplace.

This chapter provides questions that individuals and companies can use to assess where they stand in areas likely to be critical to success in the Information Age. We talk about surviving downsizing, and some things companies can do to change the contract with employees. Finally, we provide cases which illustrate three companies' approaches to improving success rates for select employees.

MEASURES OF A SUCCESSFUL COMPANY

In this section, we suggest questions that forward thinking companies and forward thinking individuals may wish to ask themselves. These questions prompt discussion about the progress that people have made, in preparing for the Information Age. These questions point to critical success factors in the changing environment we call 'work'.

How Open Is Your Information

For example, say I work as a secretary in sales. I want to know how many customers the company has, how many products the company makes, how well the company did in profits and quality scores last year, and how many clients the company lost this year and last year.

How many phone calls do I have to make to get the information? How many databases do I have to access? How many reports do I have to read? And most important of all, how many times do I get turned down?

What kind of turn downs do I get? Is it because someone at my level is not 'allowed access' to that kind of information? Is it because some executive does not have time to talk to or help out a secretary? Is it because the information is not available to anyone? Is it because data is not being analyzed? Is it because some department has the data but is 'protecting' its turf by holding on tightly to the data?

If you are an executive of a company, make a call for information, position yourself as one of the lowest grade level workers in your company, and see what you get. Analyze the reasons for lack of access to data. Congratulate the company and the appropriate systems personnel and information gatherers if the data was readily forthcoming. Encourage others in the organization, at all levels, to make inquiries and use what is available.

Where Are You In Relationship To The Marketplace—Your Suppliers And Customers?

How much time does the company collectively spend with its customers and suppliers. Add up all of the company's work hours. Add up all of the hours employees spend working with, and for, customers, suppliers and prospects.

Look at the ratio of executive time spent with customers and suppliers. Compare that to the ratio of mid level workers and below spent with customers and suppliers. Is it nearly equal. Or, is one group facing isolation from the customers and suppliers who are the purpose for the company's existence?

Look at who participates in supplier driven functions. Ask if it is only the executives who get to participate in supplier events when the function takes on social overtones. Ask if real partnerships are being built with suppliers.

Think it would be too time-consuming to gather and analyze the data? That's what computers are for—welcome to the Information Age!

Shape the organization around customers, not around internal processes. Everyone in the organization needs to be walking in the shoes of the 'folks out there'. If a particular department or team spends all or most of its time inside the company, their exposure to customer driven innovations and client-critical needs is likely to be limited. If they are outside the company, working in the customer or supplier site, collaboration and development of solutions to meet client-critical needs is likely to increase. And these client driven activities result in tomorrow's salable products and services.

If executives spend more time inside the company than outside, they are likely to be insulated from what is happening in the market. They are likely to rely on others' opinions. This, without the advantage of applying their own experience to what they might otherwise be seeing if they were out there. If executives are too proud to get their hands dirty getting to know another's business, or answering questions of subordinates, they are not as likely to capitalize on the next good idea that is out there waiting for a sponsor.

How Long Does It Take You To Respond?

Find a problem, any problem. How long does it take to investigate? How long does it take to come up with sufficient understanding to respond? How quickly can people form around the problem and begin working to understand and solve it? Can you get your suppliers and customers involved easily?

How Permanent Are The Changes You Implement?

Are you dealing with the same problems over and over again? Do you learn from your mistakes, implement change and move forward? Or, are you doomed to repeat your mistakes time and again?

What Do People Think About The Company?

Would people tell you the same things about the company if they thought you were not a key executive? Consider the example of the Prince and the Pauper: to learn about the masses, become a part of them. Shed your title, your importance, your authority. Go out and listen humbly to what others have to say.

One executive in a consulting business said his company made a point of interviewing every employee upon exit.

> It is important to understand both why an employee leaves and how she feels about the company in general. In a service business, the only tangible thing we stand on is our reputation. If that is slipping, we must be able to spot that early and intervene.
>
> One of the best early warning signals is the tenor of an exiting employee. First, he is quite likely to tell it like it is. Second, comparing comments

from one exit interview to another can point to flaws
and trends. And finally, if our people don't think
well of us, how can our customers help but see that
eventually.[1]

Who Gets Promoted? Who Gets Fired? How Are Wins Celebrated?

Look at your reward systems. Do you recognize teams or
individuals? How are salary increases and bonuses handed out?
Do you begin with a budget of available reward money and divide
it up, stopping when the budget is used? Or do you add to
rewards based upon profitability? Do you reward flexible systems
and nimble workers? Do you reward and promote people for
thinking and acting as if this were their own company? Do you
promote the risk takers or the bureaucrats?

Who Works For Whom?

Do employees work for their managers, or is the reverse the
case? How do employees rate their managers' performance? How
do managers respond?

Traditional hierarchy, which holds that workers exist to
support their bosses, is outdated and dangerous. As computers
have replaced the need for middle managers to control information
flow, they must now justify their positions by asking how they
can best help their people get work done. 360 degree feedback can
provide information on the extent to which managers understand
and support this objective. Managers must learn to participate,
rather than manage, to act, rather than to oversee, to become 'a
part of', rather than 'stand apart'. From the board on down, the
company exists because every member is empowered, and
engaged, and invested in the success of those above, below and at
the same level.

Is There A Rallying Point?

What is the focus for everyone in the company. Do all people understand and support the mission, values and purpose of the company. Do they find these to be meaningful. Are the objectives and rewards for the work they do directly tied in to the purpose, values and mission of the company? If not, why not? If so, congratulations!

How Does Communication Work?

If behavior needs to change, who is responsible for seeing that the need for change is communicated and that real change is implemented? Do employees freely contact each other, regardless of level in the organization?

Do you use e-mail communication for every employee? How much training do you give people throughout the company on how to use e-mail and information systems? Do you figure that a memo should do the trick, in terms of educating people regarding uses of e-mail? Or, do you get into the trenches and spend hands-on time helping people learn to use the number one commodity of the new era—information.

What Is Being Done About The Level Of Stress

Is the stress in your organization the kind that energizes or the kind that debilitates? As 'Scott's clone' said in the movie Starman, "You earth people are at your best when things are at their worst." Are the challenges of the organization viewed as opportunities, or are they obstacles?

> "It (environment of a corporate pressure cooker) is caused by the multitude of ways that work is done where 'the rubber meets the road' and that

over time become dysfunctional. Mending these ways has to start from the bottom up. But it will not necessarily start by itself."[2]

What Is Your Company's Tolerance For Failure?

What role do risk taking, and resulting probability of failure, play in your company?

The issue of sticking it out through tough times was discussed in an article on executives who 'bounced back' from failures. The author, Patricia Sellers, looked at the role of failure in building competence. She talked about how failure can contribute in the future to successful managers.

> "If you haven't failed yet, you probably will. And for the benefit of your career, you probably should. The rapid change that drives business today calls for unconventional thinking, action in the face of uncertainty—and occasional stumbles. . . Bill Gates, who regularly tempts failure at Microsoft, likes to hire people who have made mistakes. Says he: 'It shows that they take risks. The way people deal with things that go wrong is an indicator of how they deal with change'." [3]

What Percent Of Your Company's Revenue Is Reinvested In Training?

Who gets trained? For what purpose? Is training available to everyone?

How many hours a year do people spend in training? Does some segment of the workforce spend considerably more time in training than others? If so, why? How can you motivate others in the company to emulate this behavior?

How is training time split between task related training and building social skills and leadership styles? Are both types of training available to everyone?

How is training being used to facilitate team formation and function, to build skills and competencies within the company, in order to limit the need to search outside?

SURVIVING DOWNSIZING

In the past 10 years, downsizings have changed the way we think about the contract between companies and individuals. As 1995 comes to a close, it has been widely reported that close to 3,000,000 people have been downsized in this year alone. We have gone from prizing loyalty and longevity to supporting stockholder returns.

Downsizings are not all bad, although at the time they happen, their effect can be devastating on those they touch. Moving forward, companies and individuals must rebuild trust, based upon a new definition of co-equal, which replaces the old, hierarchical model of co-dependent.

In Downsizings Bad Things Sometimes Happen To Good People

There is not enough room for everyone, not enough income to pay everyone's salary. The conflicts of downsizing—who goes / who stays, rewards for past loyalty, shutting down of projects and businesses with potential, net loss of jobs, to name a few— lead to serious morale issues.

People who are let go are not the only ones to suffer. The ones who retain their jobs, face survivor's guilt, as well as issues about trusting the company. There may be loss of confidence in the company's ability to survive and provide growth opportunities in the future. Employees become de-motivated, depressed, and act out of fear rather than confidence. Ask any human resource manager if these are behaviors they believe will contribute to future organizational success.

Misplaced trust and loyalty, survivor guilt, fear of failure, lack of engagement, are all as debilitating to individuals as they are to companies. They are symptoms of underlying problems, but they often outwardly manifest as hostility. Except in pathological cases, people do not generally choose hostility. However they do manifest hostility when cornered or otherwise placed in situations over which they have no control, or in which they are particularly uncomfortable.

If information is not available, especially during downsizing, reasonable concerns can escalate out of proportion. Alfred Hitchcock knew better than most that fear of the unknown is nearly always greater than fear of that which is known. Individuals and companies would be well advised to keep that in mind, and to open up the flow of accurate, detailed information about what is happening and what is likely to happen. Companies need to treat their workers as adults and co-equals, not as children who must be protected from some horrible truth.

Companies Facing Downsizings Must Find New Ways To Define Success And Build Trust

If they expect to get optimum performance in the future from surviving employees, companies must re-build the trust factor.

Open communication will help, as will clarity about expectations and longevity of projects. Companies must also find another reward system besides promotions. Joining high profile teams, recognition, liberal use of appreciation, are all components.

COMPANY EMPLOYEE RELATIONS - WHAT CAN COMPANIES DO?

How do we change contracts between workers and companies. How do we engage people, and help them get over their fear of change. How do we open doors to allow each human being to contribute to the best of his/her ability. How do we help companies match individual needs with corporate goals and tasks.

> "(A) paternalistic strategy is designed to encourage blind faith and dependency among employees. It implies that you'd be taken care of with job security and a paycheck for life in exchange for your loyalty. And it worked—for awhile. Many of us considered our military-style companies to be extensions of our families. But in retrospect, real paternalism was a promise that no corporation could keep. It succeeded only in stifling creativity among workers and producing myopic thinking in American and Japanese companies. It created a system in which bold thinking was reserved solely for the CEO or a few senior executives. It helped perpetuate rigid organizational structures. It rewarded caretakers, people who were dedicated only to preserving the organization, rather than moving it ahead. And it took the focus off customers and back onto the organization.
>
> "What did it do to us employees—the heart and soul of any organization? In a very real sense, we became slaves marching to the tune of a single drummer. We started telling our bosses what we thought they wanted to hear, not what was really important. . . "[4]

We believe few people today freely choose this culture of co-dependency at work. Rather, they find themselves in the midst of an organizational structure which they feel powerless to control or to significantly alter, in which they are rewarded for conformity.

Breaking the bonds of co-dependency must become a priority for everyone within the organization, from the bottom to the top. We must learn to build strength into the organization, by strengthening the individual parts, the people who work within the organization.

> "At the organizational level, we must begin removing the hierarchical walls that we've built around us. We have to move away from close-ended organizations with independent departments that function in their own little cloistered worlds. We must move away from the concept that the boss is omnipotent and all powerful and move toward a more fluid organizational structure that favors a shared approach toward conducting business. Moreover, we have to abandon the belief that business is just a short-term proposition. It never was and never will be. . . . Values and individualism must be prized, not hidden.

The following are some of the actions companies and individuals can take, to change the contract from co-dependency to mutually supportive and respectful.

Allow Teams Time to Develop

Teams are built over time, with coaching. They don't just happen. The temptation may exist to pull back from team development, or to change tactics before the team becomes fully functional, further disrupting team formation. Remember, the standard phases of team building are: forming, storming, norming and performing. Teams will pass through each of these phases, on the way to becoming fully functional. View the occurrence of each of these steps as one more sign that the team is becoming functional.

Facilitate Development Plans

Both for union and non-union employees, various Bell Companies are placing emphasis on employees' responsibility to own the individual planning and development process. Through the company, employees have access to personal skill assessment tools, information about available jobs inside and outside the company, and background on programs that might be available to support personal development plans. Employees must do the research (by using available tools), and must initially invest personal time in plan development and training. Once a development plan is built, it is reviewed with Training and Development personnel and with Human Resources staff, as well as the individual's manager.

Position Managers' Role as Supporting Their People

Beware of the manager who 'can't work with' people he/she inherits. What does that say about the manager's flexibility and potential to work with a diverse group. What does that say about the manager's ability to encourage, coach, sustain performance. What does that say about the previous manager's judgment.

How responsible are managers and executives? As one executive commented about another,

> ". . . you know, he is certainly quick to point fingers when things fail. Why can't he be as quick to point when things succeed?"[5]

We repeatedly heard it stated, great managers celebrate the wins of their people and own the failures themselves.

Prize Employee Relations

Look everywhere in the company for measures of success or failure. If people are being treated fairly, that is likely to show in every department. If they are not, that will show too, as in the following story.

> The legal department is small for the size of the corporation. The owners want it that way. Overhead should be kept to a minimum. Everyone should be focused on doing business. The members of the legal department, like everyone else in the company, were supposed to work on new contracts and keep the company out of trouble.
>
> And then one day over coffee, David, a respected senior member of the legal staff took time to reflect on changes in the department's workload.
>
> Two years ago, we were busy, but focused. We put new business contracts first, renegotiations and supplier contracts came next, and everything else came after that. We had a lot of contracts coming in; we were writing a good chunk of new business. And we probably spent about 5% of our department's time on employee related issues. I worked long hours, but I felt productive, and I believe the others in the department did, too.
>
> Now things have changed. There has been a major shift in the time allocation in our department. It feels like we spend 50% of our time on employee related issues. I know we have tried to change some of the ways we manage people, but I wonder about the outcome. Is this really productive?[6]

Be careful of warning signs like David's comments, above. What David's department seems to be doing is unproductive. What David is talking about could mean grave danger for the company. The legal department is becoming the arbiter of situations where communication is breaking down. Once people cannot focus on common goals, share information and work out their differences, the productivity of the company begins to fall apart.

Prize Outspoken Employees

Be careful to distinguish between people who challenge the system, and people who cannot work collaboratively. In one company we interviewed, anyone who asked 'why' was labeled politically incorrect, and considered to not be a team player. In fact, many of those who challenge the system appear very capable of working on a team to create new solutions. Unfortunately, they are not given a chance to collaborate, as lack of conformity is confused with lack of cooperation.

A label of 'unsupportive,' can be a warning sign of underlying problems in the company related to control and trust. Pressure to conform, to get along, can result in doing the same thing over and over again, with the same results each time. Leaps forward come from doing things differently, looking at old problems in new ways. Changes in approach and viewpoint come from people who ask questions and challenge the status quo.

Open Information

Open information, a team approach to tackling work, and respect for everyone's ability to contribute, are critical success factors in the Information Age.

Sharing information up, down, and across the organization may reduce the need for downsizing efforts. Employees can be encouraged to move along, whether inside or outside the company, as the company communicates decisions about the value of work to be performed. Companies can further reinforce such communication with incentives for critical work and contributions to the success of the business.

With open information systems, individuals seeking growth opportunities, can query the company on its needs in the near and long term, and build skills leading to those future needs.

Reality or nightmare?

People need to be able to distinguish between real anxiety and baseless fear or concern. People must be able to gather sufficient information to determine the reality of the situation, in order to make appropriate decisions. If information is readily available, and people are encouraged to discuss the situation and collaborate on solutions, reasonable concerns can be dealt with, and unreasonable anxiety is diminished in the face of facts. If information is not available, reasonable concerns escalate out of proportion, and fear of the unknown becomes greater than that which is known.

Conscious Decisions By Employees

Companies can help employees see that careers are built by conscious decision making and by taking personal ownership of actions and outcomes.

> "Amoco Corp. established a career-management process that helps employees reflect on their marketability inside and outside the Chicago-based oil company."[7]

Companies can provide employees with the information and tools to make choices about staying, going, learning new skills and moving into new challenges, whether within the company or outside.

> "General Electric Co.'s aircraft engine manufacturing facility in Lynn, MA, has flattened itself into an enterprise where employees compete

with external providers for work. If employees can
prove to management that they can produce parts
cheaper in-house, they get the contract. . . . 'A lot of
the people today understand more of the finance
issues than do the managers,' trumpets Charles
Ruiter, business agent with the International Union
of Electrical Workers Local 201 in Lynn.

"Teams weigh materials costs, overhead,
benefits and pay as they compete with outsiders to
produce parts. 'If we win a job and get it under our
costs, is good,' says Ruiter. 'But if we lose a job, we
can analyze why we lost it.' At that point, workers
can suggest more efficient ways to operate in-house
so they have a better chance to get the next job."[8]

Make a culture of learning. Teach the workforce the
company's business, in total, not just its parts. Involve all levels
in meeting overall company objectives, and provide them with the
information to help them do so.

". . . Eastman Kodak Co. has tried to align its
career-development process with company strategy,
which involves an annual employee self-assessment
and a worker-supervisor talk about how the worker's
skills and experience fit into the big Kodak picture
for the coming year . . ."[9]

What If They Leave?

"How flexible should a company be in letting
employees pursue their own interests? . . . If they
find a hot project that really gets them going, but it's
outside the strategic plan, what do you tell them?
Sorry, not for us? Back to work on something you
don't like? . . .

"Is this good business? Says Gaither (Janet
Adams Gaither, senior organizational capabilities
consultant at Amoco headquarters in Chicago): 'If

they're really driven to do something else, they're going to do it anyway'."[10]

Some companies spend a fair amount of time worrying about whether individual employees will stay or leave. In fact, average tenure for employees at all levels, in most companies, is estimated to be less than seven years. Therefore, we suggest that companies stop worrying about whether employees may leave, and instead find ways to make certain they get optimum motivation, commitment and performance for the short time they are around.

Roles vs. Titles

When individuals come to identify themselves by the title they hold, rather than the work they do, that can be a warning sign. Titles can be shortcut descriptions. They can also take on meanings of their own. They can lock people into roles that they play, rather than emphasizing the work that they do and the value that they contribute.

Need exists within companies for people to get away from defining roles in relation to job titles. Jobs are changing quickly, resulting in a much more fluid environment. Employees are asked to take on additional responsibilities, achieve new outcomes. Doing what the person before did is likely to deliver only frustration at the same old results, and burnout over the pressure for change.

> ". . . many employees may find it necessary to rethink how work gets done and to look for ways beyond traditionally structured positions to both maximize flexibility and ensure the company is making use of the full range of employees' skills."[11]

> In companies built around assignments, *each employee has a portfolio of projects, not a job description.*[12]

It is important to define the role one will play in an organization, on a team, within a process. It is equally as important that the role definition be flexible and allow for change as skills are built and competence emerges. Job descriptions can be both good and bad—good in that they can help eliminate ambiguity and misunderstandings about expectations, bad in that they can act as boundaries on what needs to be fluid, the ability of people to contribute.

RIGHT PEOPLE, RIGHT PLACE

The following stories, gathered during interviews with companies, illustrate successful approaches to building competence and confidence in the workforce. The companies discussed are real, however they were all promised anonymity during the interviews. Their practices can be examples to others searching for models on which to build 'best practices' for creating tomorrow's workforce.

Benchmarking People to Enhance Success

One company spent considerable time helping us to understand some of their human resource practices. This company has historically operated in significant growth markets. They are a leader in their field, highly profitable, and provide above average benefits, salaries and profit sharing opportunities. For entry level management, they attract well educated, energetic people who seek a challenging environment, a few years of experience in a major industry, and a high profile name on a resume. Many of these people move on to new employers within 3 to 5 years, even more within 10 years. At the top, the pyramid is narrow, dominated by white men, populated by individuals who have spent years growing up within the business, consistently delivering above-expectation results in various lines of business and rotating job functions.

This company invests significant time and effort testing and profiling people at the manager level and above. They benchmark 'high performers', those who consistently exceed the company's standards in assigned positions. After comparing various success factors, the executive group, those the company termed the 'best of the best', rated highest in four areas:
- respect for others,
- thinking 'outside the box',
- people and organizational 'savvy' and alignment, and
- team leadership.

Fully 20 percentage points lower came categories such as:
- self confidence, and
- initiative.

Another 20 percentage points lower, or 40 percentage points below the top four success criteria, came such categories as
- integrity,
- 'analytical smarts' and
- 'customer driven'.

This company also benchmarked performers in different situations. Their first objective was to understand the success criteria of those who did well in specific situations. Their second objective was to increase the opportunity for future success in similar situations, by putting in managers with similar success characteristics, and holding back managers who did not exhibit such traits. With such an understanding, they believed they could increase individual success by targeting personnel for job rotations in which their characteristics matched the needs of the situation.

For instance, they looked at 'turn around' situations as different from other business situations. They defined 'turn arounds' as those situations, either purchased or inherited, in which the business was no longer profitable, was losing significant marketshare, or was in some way already in serious difficulty and deemed to be headed for disaster. Turn arounds are generally situations requiring rapid, dramatic leadership, and are filled with difficult, often ambiguous, trade-offs.

They found that some managers did well working in 'turn around' environments, while other otherwise successful managers failed. They found the 'turnaround leaders' excelled in two success factor areas: directiveness (ability to get to the point and 'tell it like it is') and vivid communication. This probably makes sense to most managers familiar with 'turn arounds'. After all, 'turn arounds' are situations in which there are limited time and resources available to 'stop the bleeding', and get the business back to profitability.

What we think is commendable is this company's commitment to finding the characteristics that led to success in such situations, as well as the steps they took to assure future managers assigned to such situations would have above average opportunity for success.

This company demonstrated a number of admirable traits:
- they analyzed and learned from success and failure, with the intent of changing future behavior in order to improve performance
- they recognized that all people are not the same, and that a strong manager in one situation can have a failing experience in another situation
- they recognized that appropriately matching people's success characteristics to situations requiring those characteristics increased the opportunity of success—for both the business and the individual
- they recognized that success characteristics were different from task experience, and they chose to allow managers to move beyond

task experience by focusing on matching success characteristics to business needs.[13]

Making Training Contribute to the Business

One company we interviewed had in place an internal training and development program, which they conceded was probably very expensive. Most of the program costs, while handled as line items in the training department, were ultimately charged off to operating units—from which trainees originated and to which trainees contributed while in the program. Therefore, actual costs of the program, while measured, were considered as part of the costs of doing business at the unit level.

Not isolating the costs at the training and development level was considered good. This development program contributed to the success of various business units over time. The contributions of the program were considered critical to future success of the company. The company did not consider as optional maintenance of the program.[14]

Building the Next Generation of Managers

An executive who works for a foreign based company, with major U.S. operations, talked about his company's approach to training people. Their program showed a heavy emphasis on mapping career tracks, and mentoring.

> We have a career development program, which is designed to build the company's next generation of managers and key technical workers. It is billed as a new hire training program, and we generally recruit right out of colleges.
> We assess individuals at entry level, and immediately place them on a career track. For the first six months with the company, the individual is

rotated, which enables him to gain experience and exposure to different parts of the organization. This rotation period usually lasts 24 months. After this initial period, the individual is sent to school to get an MBA, if he does not already possess one. He must also achieve fluency in the mother tongue of the organization, although that is not mandatory upon hiring. These people are assigned to high profile projects, and work with a mentor who is not their supervisor.

This management development program is considered crucial to the long-term planning of the organization. Since most of the senior management positions of the company are filled internally, it is important that we build in experience and exposure to a variety of areas of the business for executives who are likely to lead the company in the future.

We put close to 100 people into the program each year, and achieve nearly 70% in retention rate, which is higher than overall retention rates for the company. This group forms the pool for managing executives throughout the world. The program has been in place for 20 years, and we have experienced no cut backs in the program budget or initiatives, even in difficult economic times. I believe that one of the factors contributing to the success of the program is that many of our senior managers have now come from the program. They have experienced the value of the program, and understand how it can contribute to future success for the Company.[15]

Everyone Gains From Training

The companies discussed here all talked about development as a three legged stool. Employee, supervisor and company each represent one of the three legs of the stool. These companies firmly believed that all three must be committed to supporting the individual development process, even though each of the three gets something different out of it.

Gains from development programs can be classified according to the beneficiary: employer, supervisor and company. Each of these three receives something valuable and unique from participation in development programs.

Employee Gains

The employee gains an understanding of where she fits in the company, of what opportunities may become available, and of what work it may take to prepare for changes. She also gains support in developing skills, in order to change and grow.

Supervisor Gains

Through such programs, the supervisor has a vehicle for rational, fact-based discussions with the employee. The supervisor benefits by having a talented individual working for her, one who can contribute to projects. The supervisor benefits when the employee moves on to new rotations and takes away an awareness of good things that are happening in that particular area of the company. The supervisor also gets to participate in a planning process, which gives insight as to how the short and long term objectives for her department fit in with the company overall.

Company Gains

The company has a built in vehicle for sharing information and practices with others throughout the company, as the employee rotates from one department to another. The company has well trained individuals who are contributing to seamless, non-disruptive transitions. The company has a vehicle for communication with the employee an understanding of and commitment to individual development needs. Thus, when the company must ask an individual to make an extraordinary contribution, i.e. put in extra effort, stay in a job longer than desired, take a short-term assignment outside of the desired development area, the employee is more likely to participate willingly, knowing the company will move her back on track within a defined period of time. The employee is likely to spend less time worrying about the consequences of a detour, knowing the company is committed to helping individuals meet personal goals and timeframes.

SUMMARY

Companies and the people who work in them cannot continue old behaviors and expect new results. Transition to the Information Age means forward thinking people and companies have an opportunity to capitalize on change. Teams, collaboration, engagement, shared vision, all become critical success factors for tomorrow's work environment.

VI.
Promotions

Promotion has its own chapter because we found the way companies and individuals approach and manage the process says a great deal about themselves. Most of this chapter is devoted to three cases, on three separate companies. The cases are presented to illustrate how behavior can influence outcomes in employee relations and company results.

We also caution all companies that attitudes toward promotions begin, and end, at the very top of the company. What is practiced and tolerated in the executive suite, we found, flowed throughout the company. Human Resource departments can make recommendations on processes, but only the executive committee and the board can make it stick.

OBSTACLES AND ISSUES

What are some problems cited by companies in implementation of career development planning? Obstacles most often cited in our research were inability to reach agreement within the company on
- business strategies, needs and competencies, and
- how best to fill positions.

Companies having difficulty creating a vision of where they expected to be in the future, also seemed to have difficulty visualizing and creating the talent pool they need for the future.

Another obstacle cited in our research was inconsistency in senior management commitment. As priorities changed at the top, senior management's commitment to supporting development processes and programs waxed and waned. As senior management turned over, new management had their own ideas on how to develop people. They brought in their own trusted teams, despite succession plans already in place.

In the case of senior management turnover, new management has to be educated on the norms with the company—what processes are in place, and why, how they work, how they deliver results, etc. This has to happen before new management becomes committed to supporting existing programs such as development planning. Education of new management often takes over a year. Assuming programs survive the analysis stage, it can be a long time before a new, outside executive is fully up to speed and committed to supporting development programs.

Finally, establishing the value of specific programs is often subject to the selling skills of the managers in charge of the programs. Poor programs with strong advocates have a greater chance of surviving than do good programs with weak advocates. Establishing merit of programs, like most things, comes down to relationships and trust.

The following three stories illustrate very different approaches to the art of promoting employees.

PROMOTION BY BEING IN THE WRONG PLACE AT THE RIGHT TIME

The first story comes from a director of a large utility. She told about a process of job promotion which became quite convoluted. Telling how or why the company promoted anyone was hard. Merit seemed to have little to nothing to do with advancement. Being vocal seemed to play a big role.

The director who watched this story unfold was a friend of both Susan and John, the key players. Susan was a manager who was ready for a promotion, and John, her co-worker, was also ready for a promotion. This, then, is how the director told a story about getting promoted by being in the wrong place when promotions were hand out.

The company had three positions open, one in sales, one in customer service, and one in operations.

Susan's supervisor had recently moved on, and his job as sales manager was open. Susan was qualified for her supervisor's job. For the past year he had groomed her to move into that slot. She very much wanted to be the next sales manager.

Susan did not even get to interview for the job of sales manager. An outsider filled it, someone who was a friend of a senior officer of the company. Who says nepotism is not alive and well?

Meanwhile, John had already interviewed for the position in customer service, and the position in operations. John was a lot more qualified for the customer service job than the job in operations. When I heard about the story, they had already offered him the operations job. He was waiting to hear about the customer service job.

The customer service job was the one John really wanted. He felt strongly that customer service was the right job for him at this point in his career. He loved customer service.

Susan was now up in arms, having been passed over for the sales manager opportunity. She was making a lot of noise about her 'right' to move on to the next level in the company. Susan heard about the opening in customer service, and arranged to interview for it. John was a lot more qualified for the customer service job than Susan was.

Susan told me she didn't care that much about the customer service job. She just wanted a promotion. The way she put it was, if she couldn't have the sales manager job, she would have to go after something else, and the customer service manager position was open.

Susan's new manager (remember the nepotism?) recommended Susan for the position John wanted in customer service. Susan's new manager wanted her out of the department, as she viewed Susan as a competitive threat. Susan's new manager also did not want to listen to Susan's complaints about not getting promoted. Besides, as Susan's manager put it, they had already offered John the position in operations, at the same level and salary as the job in customer service.

In the end, Susan got the Customer Service Manager job. John moved to Operations, and they promised him another shot at Customer Service Manager in two years, if he did a good job in Operations. What a way to promote people!

The company had put an unqualified outsider into a key position like sales manager. The company turned a committed, productive worker into a disgruntled employee. The company then put this disgruntled employee into an equally key position in customer service, just to shut her up. Finally, the company took a guy who really wanted to do customer service and put him in operations, just because that job was the right salary and grade level. How is it that senior management wonders why it has commitment problems among their employees?[1]

Hard to believe? Unfortunately not. We heard similar stories from people in public and private companies, large and small. Remembering that promotions are about human relationships is important. They are not about moving people around like puzzle pieces, although that is certainly what happened here. Promotions say a great deal about how much companies value people, about how seriously companies take the contract between themselves and their employees.

Next we will look at another company gone awry, confusing loyalty with commitment.

LOYALTY OVER REALITY

Alice was lobbying for an assignment to a newly announced team. She felt this assignment would put her background to work, as she grew with the experience. She identified the key influencers for the assignment—members of the senior management group who were likely to have input on team member selection. She arranged to meet with each of the key influencers to discuss the opportunity.

In one meeting, she made a critical faux pas. She was asked to review her background and then answer the question of why she would want to take on the extra work of the additional team assignment. Alice repeated to us what she had said during that fateful interview.

> I want to move more into strategic planning. I feel this project would give me experience in that area. In addition, as you know, I have recently completed my MBA studies. I am used to working lots of overtime because of that effort. Now, I am looking for a new challenge. And, I want to put to use the things I studied while working on my MBA.[2]

So far, so good. Had the interview ended here, things would probably have been okay. Unfortunately, the executive who was interviewing her asked what she expected as an outcome from work on the project. In answering, she made what the executive considered a fatal mistake. Alice continued to relate her conversation from the interview.

> As I said before, I will put into practice the theories and assumptions I have from school about strategic planning. I will build real experience in the

workplace. And, I will contribute to a valuable project for the company at the same time.

Someday I do want to have my own company. The skills I might build in this project would be valuable to me in the work I would like to do someday in my own company. After all, I have about 20 years left before I want to retire from full time work, sometime in my mid 60's. I do not realistically expect to spend all of those 20 years here in this company—not many people do last to retirement around here.[3]

Alice told us what happened next.

The executive stopped her there. He admonished her, saying that her statement about leaving one day implied she was not loyal and committed to the company. He suggested that she change her story, if she interviewed with anyone else. She should say she wanted to increase her value to the company. She should leave out the part about someday leaving. He pointed out that loyalty and commitment were very important, and by talking about leaving, she was showing that she lacked in both areas.[4]

Once again, good intentions gone off track. A committed workforce is a hallmark of productive, focused companies. There is a difference between loyalty and commitment, however.

People can be very focused on and committed to the work they are doing, for the time they are doing it. They also can consider other options, including leaving the company, without jeopardizing their commitment to delivery of high quality work, on time, within budget. Thoughts of leaving a company might call in to question a person's long term loyalty, but not necessarily her commitment.

Finally, it is critical to understand and acknowledge openly that employment in Corporate America is short term—seven years on average, according to some. In a lifetime of 40 years' or more of work, seven years can seem quite fleeting. It is far more productive for employee and company to openly plan for the eventuality, rather than denying its possibility.

Now, let's look at a company that gets it right.

PROMOTION ACCORDING TO PLAN

In this illustration, the company follows an open, well documented process of job training, rotation and advancement. Each year, they evaluate employee performance. They evaluate candidates' readiness to move on to other positions.

The employee's manager participates in a coaching session with the employee. Together they make certain the employee is considering all options and looking at all potential growth opportunities realistically. From this meeting, the manager creates a profile of the employee. Then the manager meets with the President, Human Resource Officer and senior Line Manager, to review the employee profile that has been built.

Together, Manager, President, Human Resource Officer and senior Line Manager discuss each employee profile, one by one. The manager receives feedback on how they perceive the employee. The group discusses how realistic each employee's growth opportunities might be. They discuss individual readiness levels. The President, Human Resource Officer and senior Line Manager receive an education on the desires of their employees. Sometimes they can spot trends in 'hot jobs' or generalized training needs in the company.

After the senior management review session, the manager again meets one-on-one with the employee. They refine the individual development plan, to account for the employee's growth desires and the corporate views of the employee's capabilities. The employee is told who else might be competing for positions in which he has expressed interest, what education, preparation, experience will be required to move on. The employee commits to specific development activities, and the manager commits to supporting the agreed upon activities. The manager and employee develop a written description of that to which they have agreed. [5]

This process of planning facilitates open communication. It allows for information flow among all levels of the organization. It cuts down dramatically on misunderstandings about what people want to do, and as a result, builds in support for where they want to go next. The company firmly believes it contributes to a positive work environment, and to the company's continuing reputation for quality and profitability.

The company goes through this process of evaluation for about 1,300 employees annually. They admit it is time consuming. They also maintain it contributes to their continued above average success in a highly competitive industry.

WHAT IS YOUR COMPANY DOING?

Trying to figure out how much of each company applies to your working environment? One of the first questions to ask is, 'How well does anyone in the company know anyone else?'

If you don't know people outside your department or Business Unit, or three levels above or below you, how can you possibly know a lot about what is going on in the company? How can you possibly share the successes you achieve, or gain recognition for the work you are doing?

If people don't know each other, information will not flow, learning will be slower, opportunities will be missed and mistakes will be made at a greater rate than necessary.

Follow up questions for management are, 'What opportunities have you created for individuals to get to know you, and vice versa?' 'How much have you invested in learning about individuals—what they do, and how well, what they like and dislike, and what they dream about?' Follow up questions for employees include, 'What have you done to get to know those around you, including those at least two levels higher and lower in the organization?' 'Who knows what you have contributed, and what you would like to work on?'

DIFFERENT KINDS OF EMPLOYEE RELATIONS

In the first company case (the one with nepotism), employees are heard to comment that they assign people to jobs arbitrarily. Some have said that it is more important who you are than what you do, and individual contribution is not the priority when determining job assignment changes.

In the second company, values like unswerving loyalty and paternalistic management—characteristic of Industrial Age management at its height—are still practiced and promoted. Unfortunately, for this company and others like it,

> "'It's all changed since our parents made up the nation's workforce,; says Randy. 'There's no way that today's marketplace conditions can support the kind of employer/employee relationships that existed in the past. Paternalism as we experienced it from World War II until the late '80's is quickly fading into the sunset.'
> 'Market conditions today put employees and corporations at a mutual disadvantage if such a 1950s approach is implemented,' Denis observes

(Denis Sullivan and Randy MacDonald are director
and vice president for employee relations and
organizational development at GTE)."[6]

In the third company (the one with the plan), employees have
a realistic assessment of where they are, of how they fit, and of
what options and challenges lie in front of them. Employees are
encouraged to take on new challenges, learn new skills. That
activity is factored into a planning process that goes all the way to
the President.

In this company, it is incumbent on the employee and the
company together to open up opportunities so that the employee
remains engaged and committed. The employee can plan into the
future, knowing the company will support him. When employee
desires and the company's assessment of capabilities do not
coincide, employee and manager discuss it openly.

When It's Time To Move On

As the pyramid shrinks at the top, not every employee can
probably meet his or her needs inside the company. In the third
company, the one with the plan, a shrinking pyramid does not
mean the end of the employee's future in the company's eyes,
only that it may be time to move on. The company assumes that if
the employee has made a contribution up to now, she will
continue to have potential and contribute in the future, whether
inside the company or outside. Employees do not 'drift away', nor
does the company lose interest in its people simply because an
employee's focus lies outside the company. Managers in the
company play a role in the transition, both to the next job inside
the company, and, when the time comes, to work outside the
company.

This company should be applauded for the courage and
foresight to work openly on the process of employee development,
planning for eventual transition cooperatively.

Competitive Threats

This third company also talked about competitive threats. Employees are considered skilled knowledge workers. This company does have a number of competitors. This company's employees are considered valuable by the competition. Yet, this company has had little problems with losing employees to competitors.

When an employee leaves the company, it is usually because an opportunity is available outside that would not be expected to open up within the company. Often in these cases, the employee will end up with a supplier or customer. Sometimes they form a joint venture. The employee identifies a niche or market needs that she wants to pursue. The company agrees to out source related work to the employee, and helps to partner the employee with customers or suppliers in order to get started.

> "The possibility of training workers only to see competitors steal them away has always been a concern in the business world. . .
>
> "'That concern doesn't stop Hewlett-Packard from training people in highly portable skills, however. And H-P has always had one of the lowest turnover rates in the electronics industry," says Davis.
>
> ". . . if a company provides a lot of training and learning opportunities, it is more likely to retain workers because it creates an interesting and challenging environment. As Davis put it, 'What is going to entice them away? Money? Maybe you can buy them for a short term, but what keeps people excited is growing and learning.'
>
> ". . . Berlo (Dave Berlo, founder of The Berlo Programs, a St. Louis consulting firm) suggests that the ideal corporate environment would be one in which everyone in the organization is there, not because they have to be, but because they believe it's

the best game in town. As far as Berlo is concerned,
any CEO who says he can't afford to train his
employees because the competition might steal them
away is admitting that people wouldn't work for his
company if they had any other choice."[7]

In the first company, people stay because they know they
won't be fired; it is a job and they are safe if they keep
performing adequately. In the second company, people hesitate to
'put it on the line'. In the third company, people stay because they
are engaged. They know and understand the two-way contract.

MAINTAINING MORALE WHEN PROMOTIONS ARE GONE

How does one maintain morale with fewer slots? Companies
and employees need to own up to a few realities of today's
workplace. First, it is unlikely that more than a few employees
will stay with a single company for their entire work lives. Or,
conversely, it is likely that most employees will leave the
company before retirement. Companies and employees would do
well to discuss this likelihood openly, and to plan for that
eventuality, to obtain maximum benefit from each other while
together. Instead, companies and employees generally are afraid
to discuss the possibility of separation, fearing that one or the
other will take offense, and will stop investing in the relationship
prematurely. By avoiding discussion of eventual separation, we
believe individual and company risk greater losses of
productivity, investment and commitment, than if they were to
deal with the subject upfront.

What a difference it would make if company and employee
would take time each year to look critically at contribution, merit,
worth, value and assess the one, two and five year horizons.

Many companies say they do this; many employees say they don't.

This approach of regular assessment and planning assumes honesty, openness, willingness to address problems and successes. Manager and direct report must treat each other with respect, as team members and contributors. They must convert discussion of work to task-based review and planning. Success and failure parameters need to be defined. The question, 'What else could be done to improve' needs to be asked and answered.

Perhaps to some this seems like basic management. How often and how widely is this behavior practiced in your environment? How straightforward are the discussions? How honest are the answers? Most of us may know better, but do we take the time to carry out the very actions we say we need to do? How often does 'review time' become a rote process, filling in boxes on a form to file with personnel? What if reviews became times to honestly own up to what is going on in the company. For individuals, what if reviews became times to share dreams about the future without constraints of loyalty and tenure.

Bear in mind what seems to happen when someone performs the same function year after year, without challenge, stimulation or additional responsibility. Stagnation sets in. He becomes less involved, takes less initiative, puts forward fewer suggestions, operates by rote. These behaviors are not going to help the company make great leaps forward improving processes, doing work 'easier, faster and better.' Productivity in the company is likely to slow as employees turn elsewhere, outside the work environment, for stimulation and growth. The company loses productivity, probably not knowing why, how or where. As productivity turns down, profit margins shrink, customer satisfaction may diminish, and finally profitability is in jeopardy. Then comes downsizing, just to survive.

We are reminded of the children's story about losing the horseshoe, horse, rider, message, battle, war, and kingdom, all for want of a horseshoe nail. Honest communication, open and scheduled review of company and individual performance and expectations, planning for exit to the next job, involvement of every employee in decision analysis and problem resolution related to sales, operations and profitability are like horseshoe nails.

VISION FOR THE INFORMATION AGE

Imagine a workplace where each quarter each employee defines how many hours of work he or she can put in, balancing priorities inside and outside of the workplace. Imagine that such behavior is encouraged, allowing employees to put in more or less effort and output, on a contract basis. Imagine adjusting compensation and access to additional opportunities accordingly. Imagine the employee making conscious choices about his or her work, home life, and other commitments. Imagine that earnings and growth opportunities are part of a deliberate process of choices, rather than accidents.

Imagine an environment in which company and individual make a job contract for a specific period and work task. Both parties agree as to expectations, penalties in case of failure, and payoff for delivery along the way and at the end of the assignment.

During, and especially toward the end of an assignment the individual budgets time to identify new projects on which to work when this job is complete, or renegotiates to extend the current project, if appropriate. If the individual is providing valuable work, the company may decide to continue; if not, the company should provide feedback that the project will be ending, or will not be extended. If the individual is pleased with the work environment and the quality of projects on which she is working, she will probably choose to stay. If she does not feel comfortable or fulfilled, she, too, is free to provide feedback that she will leave at the end of the project.

Together, individual and company measure the value of the work performed, provide feedback to each other as to changes that need to be made, adjust the budget, if necessary, to account for the merit of the work (above or below expectations) and the speed required to complete the project (ahead or behind schedule). Teamwork.

VII.
The Entrepreneurial Class

SMALL BUSINESS

A dramatic shift is underway from large corporate environments to small businesses. All levels of our workforce, from company presidents to factory workers are making the transition. Some people are embracing the change, anticipating greater control and freedom; others fear the challenges and loss of structure, benefits and perks.

> "In 1992, Bill Clinton won the White House on the strength of a blunt, but effective, campaign slogan: 'It's the economy, stupid.' Almost three years later, the president and his advisors now find themselves struggling to explain why an economy that looks so strong on paper feels so flimsy to many Americans . . . The problem is that, economically speaking, the country is in good shape. . . . But that is little consolation to full-time . . . workers . . . An air of insecurity hovers over blue- and white-collar workers, alike, making them afraid to ask for raises or leave their jobs to pursue better-paying ones."[1]

Change is difficult. We strongly believe that some part of the insecurity felt by today's American workforce is due to transitions to which we are all exposed

- from Industrial Age to Information Age,
- from hierarchy-bound job descriptions to team based projects,
- from security of large corporate surroundings to free flying environments of small business and independent work.

Whether we are ready or not,
> "By year's end (1996), many businesses and
> industries will begin to appreciate keenly both how
> vulnerable they are to new forms of competition—
> and how great the opportunities are for those who
> welcome the future rather than resist it."[2]

No matter their readiness, for a major segment of the
American workforce, work in small business either already is, or
within the next few years will be, a reality.

Small businesses' ultimate manifestation is the home office.
The shift to home office work was summed up well by Barbara
Pagliuca, Realtor for Siderow Associates, in Chappaqua, New
York. Chappaqua historically has been a bedroom community —
filled with middle and upper middle class commuters to New
York City.

> You know, it is amazing to me, as I go into
> houses today, in every price range, how many of
> them have offices in the home—from low budget
> homes to the million-dollar price range. We see the
> primary breadwinner, and sometimes both spouses,
> maintaining apparently successful businesses out of
> the house.
>
> A few years ago we rarely saw that. It used to
> be that the only reason people worked out of the
> house was because they had been laid off. They were
> working out of the house to find another job. The
> home-office set up was temporary.
>
> Now, many of these home offices are obviously
> serious business endeavors, run by experienced
> business people. We see big homes, clearly with
> large upkeep expenses, and find that people are
> making enough money in their home businesses to
> support the lifestyle. These people are making a
> deliberate, different choice about work and lifestyle.
>
> Telecommuting, no getting stuck in the snow,
> being home to see the children and enjoy the
> surroundings you own—sounds great to me![3]

WHAT IS THE FUTURE FOR SMALL BUSINESS?

Given small businesses' positive contribution to job creation, their success is critical to the well-being of the American economy. Small business represents a major sector of the business community. For example, in New York State, they make up 96% of all businesses operating in the state.[4]

In this chapter, we look at some facts about small businesses, and also some of their opportunities and challenges. We look at the transition from corporate worker to entrepreneur, including the critical importance of changing role definition. And we look at steps that an individual must be willing to take, building skills and nurturing qualities, to ensure a continued livelihood in the Information Age.

Regarding small businesses, it has been written that:
"Their economic outlook is positive. Their expectations for growth are the highest in four years. Their access to capital has improved. And, their challenges to growth and survival have abated, somewhat.
". . . However, amidst an improving economic landscape, there are several significant challenges."[5]

The challenges facing Small Businesses include coping with government regulations and tax laws, obtaining financing, attracting and retaining a diverse workforce, building skills, and most important of all, defining successful roles for all members of the company. Further on in this chapter, we touch on these challenges, to better understand the problems associated with them. But first, let's define Small Business.

DEFINITION OF SMALL BUSINESS

Some define small business as companies with less than 100 employees. Other reports and surveys classify statistics on companies with less than 500 employees as 'small business' (approximately 20 million businesses in 1995 employ less than 500 employees). Still other reports differentiate between incorporated and unincorporated business.

For the purposes of this book, we consider as small business any unit of one or more persons, performing work in the business arena. We have not tried to define the upper limit of the population. A company with 1,000 employees might consider itself 'small', in comparison to a company with 100,000 employees or more. We believe that many issues presented in this book will affect businesses in different ways, and to varying degrees, as they grow in size.

We do talk about 'large businesses' throughout this book as different from small business. Large business we have loosely and intuitively defined as companies

- with sufficient resources and capital to sustain themselves through multiple downturns or crises,
- with a history of operation, and
- which have built a sizable employee population resulting in the need to focus significant resources on management of that employee population, separate and distinct from issues surrounding operation of the business.

In other words, large businesses are those organizations that have moved beyond a total focus on business and are now focusing significant effort on managing people, past experience and internal resources.

It is not our intent to label small or large business as 'good' or 'bad'. We do look at barriers to formation of small businesses, and opportunities smallness gives rise to in the Information Age.

SMALL BUSINESSES MATTER!

Using the Small Business definition of less than 500 employees, Arthur Anderson and NSBU cite the following statistics on U.S. small businesses.

- two-thirds of initial jobs are provided by small business
- from 1987 to 1993, small businesses accounted for the U.S.'s net new jobs
- small businesses further add to jobs by heavy use of outsourcing: 64% have outsourced operations to outside suppliers, particularly in specialty fields of accounting, payroll processing and benefits/insurance
- they provide work for nearly 60% of American workers
- this group provides basic on-the-job training skills
- 52% of all sales and half of private sector product in the U.S. come from small business
- their numbers have increased by 49% since 1992
- from 1992 to 1995 (forecast), small businesses have seen continued growth of revenues, gross profits, employees and employee compensation
- small businesses are reinventing revenue growth in the workforce in the form of increased employee compensation,

particularly in companies with heavy R&D investments[6]

LEADERSHIP CHARACTERISTICS

"The small and mid-sized businesses that grew the fastest during the past 12 months are planning larger than average investments in R&D, marketing, training and new technology[7]."

The growth leaders also offered more of all benefits, including bonuses, profit sharing and ESOPs.

Technology

While investments in training, research and development, and new technologies (including computers) appear to be success indicators, 30% to 50% of small businesses plan in the next 12 months to make NO investment in each of these areas.[8]

This is a concern, as small businesses need to be encouraged to continue investments in training, research and development and new technology, to continue to grow.

Computers

Distinguishing factors for growth leaders included use of computers.

"Only 2% of companies that increased their workforce by 10% or more last year did not use computers, as compared to 19% of all companies. Overall, fast-growing companies were more likely than average to have computers, upgrade their computers systems, access the Internet and use an on-line service."[9]

Small businesses must automate, rapidly. Ability to process information and ability to respond rapidly to changing needs grow in importance as American business transitions to the Information Age. Small businesses that are computer literate will be favored with opportunities.

Management Style

Small Businesses tend to have more open management structures. They tend to be less likely to emphasize hierarchy. As workers handle a range of tasks, from opening the mail to signing major contracts, most workers and management are likely to be in contact with customers. In addition, the need to shift from task to task, driven by a limited ability to support excess overhead, means more variety in work performed and probably results in greater flexibility of work style. These factors, open structures, variety, getting close to customers, flexibility, are success characteristics of the Information Age.

Diverse Workforce

To be optimally competitive, small businesses must attract the best workers—regardless of background, race or gender. In addition, minorities and women are likely to seek opportunities in small business environments. They may seek to gain control over their environment by working as closely as possible to the business owners. Or, they may choose to become owners themselves, and then become role models for others like themselves.

Businesses are likely to attract and retain a higher caliber workforce if they can pass beyond barriers of bias, and reward team members fairly, regardless of background, gender or color. Minorities and women continue to move from large to small businesses. They are frustrated over inequities they have seen and experienced. They resolve to operate differently once they are in control. Therefore, we expect to see small businesses, often run by minorities and women, exhibit greater sensitivity to dealing with bias and rewards.

Team Collaboration

When compared to large businesses, we believe minority and women business owners are more likely to understand the importance of team collaboration. Women in particular have been trained to behave differently. This training is an advantage in small businesses in the Information Age.

> "Rosener's 1990 study of International Women's Forum members, published in the *Harvard Business Review* examined the leadership style of successful women—an 'interactive' model, in which women worked to have positive interactions with others. The 'women encourage participation, share power and information, enhance other people's self-worth, and get others excited about their work.' This leadership style, Rosener concluded, emerged because of the socialization and career paths taken by these women. Rosener later reveals what may be equally important: Most of the women surveyed worked for medium-sized, fast-growing companies or organizations, suggesting that traditional, large-scale companies may not have been as receptive to this new female leadership style."[10]

Women and minorities are more likely to support and encourage collaboration of individuals from diverse backgrounds. Diversity among team members has been shown to result in broader solutions to complex problems. Complex problems are the norm for the Information Age. Competitive advantage goes to those teams and firms able to rapidly develop superior solutions.

Open Information

As we transition to the Information Age, access to information and ability to process data increase potential for complexity and variety.

"Millions of people will have their first experiences with the mind-boggling potential of interactive networks overflowing with interesting information."[11]

Broad sources of information and complex problems, typical in the Information Age, will benefit from the perspective and collaboration of a diverse workforce. Teams who understand and value diversity in all aspects of work are likely to contribute most greatly to future business success.

Independent Workers

Small business owners, often renegades themselves, are likely to prize independent workers. And,

"Robert Waterman, whose most recent book is *What America Does Right*, says that independent employees are good for a company because they tend to tell it like it is."[12]

Being in touch with reality, and having a pulse on rapid changes and their impacts on the business, mean small businesses are more likely to remain current and avoid obsolescence.

ROLE OF FINANCING

Access to finances is one of the most critical issues any business faces. Small businesses are particularly vulnerable when access to financing is limited. They tend to take less conventional approaches to obtaining financing, as compared to large business models, particularly in the smallest businesses and in the start-up years. According to a survey of small businesses:

- 23% of businesses felt they had not obtained adequate financing, and
- 17% attributed lack of growth or expansion to inadequate financing.
- Top two targeted uses of capital were investments in plant or equipment and hiring of new employees—essential components that fuel overall economic growth.

"Small and mid-sized businesses that obtained adequate financing were significantly more likely to report increases in revenues, profits and employees over the last 12 months than those with inadequate financing."[13]

The average percentage increase in revenues was more than three times as great in adequately financed companies.

60% of small and mid-sized business (companies with less than 500 employees) did not use bank loans for financing in the last 12 months. In businesses with less than 20 employees, 70% used some form of financing in the previous 12 months. Venture Capital was one of the least used forms of financing; most heavily used forms of financing were credit cards, and private loans and/or personal bank loans.[14]

In other words, small businesses need financial assistance, but do not rely on traditional sources of financing used by their larger counterparts.

Small businesses are likely to be highly sensitive to overall economic conditions. To ensure survival, they are likely to swiftly start countermeasures when downturns in revenues and profits are felt. Therefore, as more business is concentrated in small businesses, we are likely to see increased speed of response to spikes in economic cycles. When downturns occur, small businesses may quickly lay off employees and cut expenses as fast as possible. According to the Survey of Small and Medium Sized Business, the number one significant challenge to growth and survival is a recessionary environment, particularly in companies in the North East and the West.[15]

NEW BUSINESS = NEW PRODUCTS & SERVICES

The younger the company, the more likely it is to have developed a new product or service in the past 12 months. Just over half of small and mid-sized businesses open for 0-3 years developed new products or services in the past year. By the time they were open for 11 or more years, innovation had fallen off. Less than one in three businesses open 11 or more years developed new products or services in the past year.[16]

Clearly, as entrepreneurs step out of other companies to pursue a dream or a new idea, they have a focus of purpose around bringing a new product or idea to market. Those concerned with American business are challenged to support these new entrepreneurs, to ensure the United States' position as an innovator in the worldwide market.

BENEFITS, TAX RELIEF AND ADMINISTRATIVE COSTS IN SMALL BUSINESSES

Barriers will only slow the economy and slow job formation. We must recognize the obstacles to small business, and remove them as rapidly as possible, in order to support our competitive position in the global marketplace.

Barriers To Competition For Small Business

As business people transition out of large businesses, they find a complex set of tax laws await them in the small business environment.

One woman who, along with her husband, has chosen to practice her profession out of her home, talked about the tax issues they faced.

> We both have offices in the house. Two of the eight rooms in the house are used solely for business—that's 25% of the house.
> Before I and my husband worked out of the house, no one was home during the day. Now, as a result of working out of the house, we have to heat and air condition the house all the time. Our lights are on day and night. We run computer and other office equipment constantly. The fuel bill is up significantly. The monthly electric bill has nearly doubled. The cleaning person is here an extra hour every week, cleaning rooms that we use only for business.
> My husband, besides having an office in the house, has a second office with many clients an hour away. He drives to the second office nearly every day, for part of the day, and this costs him 100 miles per day on the car, plus $6 in tolls. That adds up to an average additional expense of $6,000 per year. He begins and ends each day upstairs, in his office in our home, which is where he maintains his records.
>
> Thanks to the tax laws on home based offices, we cannot deduct any of this. Our big business counterparts routinely deduct the costs of real estate,

electricity, heat, cleaning and travel from office to office.

I have considered getting office space in town, just to solve the tax issue. Particularly for my husband, we would come out ahead financially, if he moved his office out of the house into town. However, one reason we operate the way we do is for convenience—and it is much more convenient to work out of the house.

We can get things done at all hours by working out of the house. We don't struggle with remembering to bring files home to work on. Our clients know they can reach us when they need to do so. I just don't think tax law should penalize us for operating this way. [17]

The situation this woman describes represents a real barrier to competition for small business. Home based businesses are one of the fastest growing segments of the American economy. Tax law is taking an uneven bite out of their profits and operating costs, as compared to the rules imposed for non-home-based businesses.

The Small Business Administration is pressing for legislative changes to decrease administrative burdens on small businesses,

"Small companies spend up to 80% more per employee complying with federal regulations than big companies spend, a Small Business Administration study showed."[18]

Working with the SBA are lobbying organizations focused on small businesses, such as National Federation of Independent Business and National Small Business United. These organizations represent some of the collective bargaining organizations of the future, as small business owners and individuals look for representation at the state and national level.

Benefit And Administration Costs

Non-business related costs for benefits and administration are significant, particularly for small businesses. Costs for services related to these tasks are often subject to negotiation. For example, a large company or group can negotiate significantly lower health care and dental care premiums than a single individual.

As individuals leave large company employment, they must still deal with administrative tasks. As individuals, with limited bargaining power, they are likely to pay much higher costs for equal or less service, as compared to their former employers. As small business owners, they face complex administrative and tax barriers.

Health Care Inequities

Self-insured health plans have become a tool of large business to avoiding government limitations at the state level. Self insured health plans are exempted from state regulation by the Employee Retirement Income Security Act (ERISA). This allows large companies to avoid provision of specific benefits mandated at the state level. Small businesses remain subject to state mandates on health care provisions. They do not have the pool of employees or other administrative means to create and manage self-insured health plans. The net effect is steeper health care costs for the small businesses—or no health care at all. NSBU recommends that Congress should extend the ERISA pre-exemption of state mandates to small business in order to level the playing field with large businesses in the provision of health care plans for their employees.[19]

Health Care Deductions

For individuals, tax deductions for health care are limited to 30% of their health care insurance costs. Companies (incorporated businesses) can deduct 100%. This 30% is actually up from 25% a year ago, thanks in part to lobbying efforts by organizations such as the National Federation of Independent Business. Rules of incorporation are sufficiently complex and expensive as to limit the value of incorporating simply to qualify for health care deductions. This issue grows in importance as companies increase deductibles and co-payments to control the cost of insurance premiums. Increasing deductibles and co-payments mean individuals must cover more health care expenses out of their own pockets.

Fears of Lost Benefits

Ellen shared with us her concerns about health care coverage. She was leaving a large company to start her own business. Her husband, Tom, was also an entrepreneur, and had been out on his own for five years. Up to now, they had relied on Ellen's company for medical insurance. Now all that would change.

They were taking considerable risks and would incur significant expenses, from a medical standpoint, according to Ellen.

> Medical coverage is probably the thing I worry about most, when I think of starting my new business. Isn't that crazy? You would think I would be most worried about finding my first customer, or having enough operating capital, or building a good public relations campaign.
>
> But, I worry most about medical insurance. You see, Tom has a long term, degenerative heart

condition. He is fine now, able to work and live a pretty normal life—except that we have a lot of expenses for doctor visits and medications.

I will be eligible for insurance coverage from my current employer for the next 18 months, under COBRA (Consolidated Omnibus Budget Reconciliation Act). But after that, any new insurance plan is probably going to exclude Tom's expenses for the first 12 months, because it's a 'preexisting condition.'

I don't even want to think about what it is going to cost us to pay for coverage that will allow Tom to continue treatment with the specialists he sees now. Assuming we can get coverage, the monthly premiums will be at least twice what I and my current employer, together, pay for health care insurance today. I feel like Tom and I are going to be flying without a parachute within six months.

Leaving my current job feels incredibly risky. But I don't feel I have any real alternative. The corporate environment is just not safe anymore, either. I would rather get out now, with a plan, before I get caught in some round of downsizing and am pushed out anyway.

I used to think big government social programs were undesirable. Big Brother, inefficient, wasteful, and all that. Now I pray for universal health care. I would love to have the government get involved in containing insurance costs and coverage conditions, so that Tom and I can afford the care we need. And yes, I do recognize there could be a down line trade off limiting access to care in later stages of Tom's disease. However, I don't see it as much of a trade off, since I can't imagine how we'll pay for that care anyway, given today's insurance market conditions.[20]

We believe that Ellen has hit on a key issue for many individuals considering the transition from employee to entrepreneur. The company has generally provided an umbrella of care. The company's costs to provide care are lower than the individual's because of its negotiating leverage and the ability to spread risks across a pool of employees.

Benefits do appear to be eroding steadily in many large as well as small companies. The resulting economic pressure falls directly to individual workers. The fall off in benefits includes regular pay, loss of annual salary increases, fewer paid holidays, higher health care premiums and larger deductibles and co-payments.

> "At Wal-Mart Stores Inc., only 41% of its workforce actually got health insurance through the company in 1993. . . . 'If Wal-Mart isn't providing decent benefits, how can you expect smaller retailers to do better?' says Greg Denier, a spokesperson for the 1.4 million member United Food & Commercial Workers Union."[21]

More and more households have at least one member working entrepreneurially. They may not have access to two insurance plans. Instead, the entrepreneurial member relies on the umbrella of the other member who works for an employer offering various benefits. As benefit coverages fall off, the household directly incurs the additional costs, which then reduce total household net income. Dual working households cannot make up for all of this benefit fall off.

Pension Plans

Pension Plan administration and regulations governing participation are not simple. According to the National Federation of Independent Business and to National Small Business United, only 24% of employers with less than 100 employees currently provide pension plans. This becomes a competitive disadvantage, as small businesses compete for workers with large companies, which are able to amortize administration costs over a bigger population. There is growing pressure on Congress to simplify the rules. A 1995 initiative, introduced by Republican Robert Dole, is named, appropriately enough, SIMPLE.

Tax And Other Government Regulations

Currently, taxes and government regulations represent an uneven playing field, when individual workers and small business owners compete against large businesses. Barriers to entry and brakes on operations for independent workers and small business owners include: differences in health care deductions, home office deductions, pension plan rules, and rules for independent contractors.

Small and mid-sized businesses report payroll and tax filing/deposit requirements as the most significant regulatory burden on their business.[22]

Home Office Deductions

Rules governing home office deductions are very complex and highly restrictive. If time is spent out of the home based office meeting with clients (which is where time should be spent if we are to follow the admonition to get close to the customer), current rules make it difficult to take deductions for home office expenses. In other words, an office is not always an office—particularly if it is in the home. Ellen's story earlier in this chapter illustrates some of the frustrations home office workers are likely to feel regarding the inequities of tax treatment.

Imagine the uproar in big business if companies were told they could not deduct office space expenses anytime workers left to spend time with clients and colleagues.

According to National Small Business United,

"A recent Supreme Court ruling eliminated almost all office-expense deductions for home-based businesses. The ruling unfairly discriminates against these companies by taxing them for legitimate business expenses that larger companies can deduct.

". . . . The U.S. Supreme Court, in the 1993 decision *Commissioner of Internal Revenue v. Soliman,* placed stringent criteria on the definition of 'principal place of business.' Under the ruling, a consultant or contractor who uses his residence as an office but who actually performs services at other locations—such as clients' offices—cannot deduct the expenses of the home-office. [23]

Independent Contractors

When it comes to regulations on independent contractors, both business owners themselves and employees of many small businesses, face complex, some say inconsistent, rulings from the Internal Revenue Service (IRS).

According to NSBU,

"The Internal Revenue Service (IRS) is ambiguous and inconsistent in applying Independent Contractor classification standards. When the IRS rules that an employer misclassified an employee as an independent contractor, the employer is liable for thousands of dollars in fines, back taxes and benefits.

"In recent years, the IRS has become increasingly aggressive in contesting the classification of some independent contractors. The agency audits businesses that utilize independent contractors, looking for reasons to reclassify those workers as employees. A reclassification can result in tax assessments going back as far as three years per 'employee'. In addition, the IRS often imposes stiff fines on the employer for each misclassified worker. The employer also may be held responsible for the value of past employee benefits, such as health insurance and pension plans.

"Section 530 of the Revenue Act of 1978 created a safe-harbor for many businesses employing independent contractors, but the provision is not clearly understood or consistently enforced. Since its original inception, the confusion over the safe harbor has only increased."[24]

NSBU Recommendations

"The (federal) administration should direct the Treasury Department to draft a reasonable, understandable standard for determining independent contractor status. A new safe harbor should be clear and iron-clad. Failing such executive action, Congress should amend the law to effect this. The new standard should limit penalties resulting from inadvertent misclassifications in cases where there is no evidence of fraud."[25]

Issues surrounding independent contractor classification also affect large businesses. However large businesses generally have more access to legal and accounting representation, which are crucial to limiting charges and penalties. Small businesses have finite funds to allocate to challenging an IRS ruling. The effort of challenging an IRS ruling represents an order of magnitude drain on the resources of small companies, as compared to their larger counterparts.

Independent contractor status is an option for many workers. Changes of the Information Age favor project-based work. As a result, individual workers move from company to company. Consequently, it can be expected that Independent Contractor ranks will swell, as individuals identify their work as separate from a specific company. Difficulty with IRS rulings on

Independent Contractor status is likely to create barriers to entry and continuation of work, in some situations.

TRAINING IN SMALL BUSINESSES

According to survey by National Small Business United, a national small business advocacy group, one in five small businesses ranked training and recruiting qualified workers
". . . as the most significant challenge to their (small business) future growth and survival."[26]

Since small businesses account for more than 90% of all new job creation in the United States, we must assume that many small businesses give workers entry level opportunities. Yet the cost of providing training can be prohibitive in a small business with limited financial resources. In addition,
"Federal worker training initiatives target displaced workers from specific industries, sometimes even from specific companies. The process tends to neglect people who work for or have worked for small business[27]

RE-DEFINING SELF AND WORK

Today, for Information Age individuals, pride in work replaces pride in title. Contribution to projects becomes a success measure. We must move away from a dependent marriage to employer in favor of a
". . . more self reliant model in which both parties are equal. . . . Too often, Noer (Dave Noer, vice president of training and education at the Center for Creative Leadership in Greensboro, NC and author of *Healing the Wounds: Overcoming the Trauma of Layoffs and Revitalizing Downsized*

Organizations) says, 'we force people to put a lot of their social and emotional eggs in the organizational basket'."[28]

The importance of one's view of oneself is discussed by John A. Thompson. John was Chairman of KMG Main Hurdman in the mid 1980's. John was downsized in 1988. In the preface to his book, 'The Portable Executive,' he writes,

> "January 1, 1988, was the first day since I graduated from college that I did not have a job. The feelings of emptiness, loneliness, worthlessness, and above all, 'fear' sent me into a tailspin for the next few months. And I was angry. After all, I had done everything that was expected of me, and I had done it well. But I was fifty-three years old, and jobless.
>
> "With two children still in college, I immediately began preparing my résumé and talking to headhunters. . . The pressure I put on myself to find a job was, in some part, economic, but it was also related to my self-esteem. I felt that I was no good unless I was working.
>
> " . . . I had never realized how afraid I was to break the mold and stray from that plan I had set for myself in my younger years (to be a partner in a national accounting firm). And I would never have believed that I would leave the analytical nonentrepreneurial, nonpersonal world of public accounting to start my own company in the intuitive, interpersonal work of placing interim managers."[29]

John then went through a personal searching process,
> " . . . that helped me to understand that my value was not dependent on KMG Main Hurdman or any other organization I would work for. My value, I discovered, resided wholly within myself."[30]

BUILD SKILLS AS FAST AS YOU CAN

In the Epilogue, 'Sarah Doesn't Work Here Anymore,' Sarah describes an important change she had made between her first and second downsizing experiences. She was willing to go back to school, to learn, to enhance existing skills and to build new skills. Thompson, too, talks about this need.

> "Since their core skills are both their greatest asset and their entire inventory, portable executives must learn that developing and maintaining them is *not* an optional investment. . . . it is critical for you as a portable executive to view skill maintenance and development as an investment in the quality of your business, and to allot sufficient resources for it. Otherwise, you're apt to find another portable executive with up-to-date skills snatching your market share."[31]

To this end, individuals must take steps to build skills, to ensure a continued livelihood in the Information Age. Going to the lengths Sarah describes in the Epilogue is probably not necessary. There are many alternatives to investing one to two years, or more, in obtaining an MBA, if you do not already have one. Continually updating and expanding skills is critical, to remain current and marketable.

WHICH SKILLS TO BUILD?

Decide what skills to develop, and to what extent. There are at least three steps to the process of skill building:

- The first step is spending time to understand the critical needs of organizations and individuals.

- The second step is being willing to seek out learning, to better understand issues related to critical needs.
- The third step is being flexible enough to study new areas, to build a sufficient base of skills surrounding a wide variety of critical needs.

First Step

Start by spending time to understand the critical needs of organizations and individuals. To obtain information on what skills to develop, ask co-workers, clients and prospects what are their critical needs. Needs turn into unsolved problems, which usually go unsolved because of insufficient time, or expertise, within the company. In either case, an unfulfilled critical need is an opportunity. Whether as an employee or as an independent worker, showing a way to solve critical needs of companies is a sure way to secure work and earn income.

Second Step

Be willing to seek out learning, to better understand issues related to critical needs.

So many employees today do not take time out from work to go to school. Many companies will not allow time off from work, or pay for skill development. Many individuals say that if the company will not contribute, they are not going to make the effort. This is short sighted. Individuals lacking continued skill development are likely to be left behind in the race to differentiate and build value.

Third Step

Be flexible enough to study new areas, to build a sufficient base of skills surrounding a wide variety of critical needs.

Some people approach the issue of skill development across a very narrow horizon. They may say, 'I am an expert at X; if it is Y, I don't do that.' Such behavior is very dangerous, given the speed of change in the Information Age. Today's experts can easily become tomorrow's buggy whip manufacturers.

Attempting to portray oneself as an expert in a specific area without doing sufficient homework can be equally dangerous. Demand for 'doing it right the first time' is very high, and the margin for error is always shrinking, as information moves quickly and decisions are made rapidly.

WHAT QUALITIES TO NURTURE?

To succeed in the Information Age, there is also a need to build balance between three qualities:
- generalist,
- researcher, and
- subject expert.

Balancing these three qualities can become an art, as the Information Age worker must employ all three qualities, to different degrees, at different times. Building the skills, flexibility and qualities of learning, can become differentiating success factors for individuals making the transition from Industrial Age to Information Age.

Generalist

Successful individuals must know something about a variety of topics and issues. If you are not already there, start learning FAST. This quality includes developing a real curiosity about things you do not already know. It includes being willing to listen to others. Cruise the Internet, spend time at the library, hang out in computer stores, listen to radio and television, read newspapers, magazines and books—however you best locate and absorb new information, just do it!

Researcher

Next, you must know where to find information. Start with your library, join associations, join support groups, network, check out the local community college, visit the nearest university. Have ready access to information. Share information, trade opinions. Know that information is a prize commodity as we leave the Industrial Age.

Subject Expert

Finally, once a need for expertise is determined to exist, be willing to put in sufficient time and effort to become a temporary expert. Computers are wonderful for this.

> "You can become an instant expert on practically any subject through the use of databases, bulletin boards, and on-line networking capabilities that give you access to libraries throughout the world and to almost every major international publication."[32]

It is important to know enough about a subject or issue, to be able to give sound advice and make sound judgments, upon which later decisions and actions can be based. Having too shallow an understanding of a subject can be like building a house on a foundation of sand.

HERE'S TO TOMORROW!

"Any company that hopes to be competitive in the 21st century may want to consider creating a Collaborative Workplace. In these times of instability and chaos, it is not only the most efficient form of organization for a highly networked marketplace, but also the most effective way to engage the members of the workforce and enable them to be their most productive selves. Even more important, it brings dignity, civility, and values-based stability to the workplace.

"The past, however, is no longer prologue. We cannot create the future by reengineering the past. To forge a new path into the 21st century, we must now seize the opportunity to transcend our current way of thinking about leading and managing businesses. The intention of this book has been to define that pathway.

"It is time to stop looking for the silver bullet to resolve complex organizational issues. It is time to move beyond the quick fix. It is time to truly transform our organizations, to face the paradox head-on, and to bring peace and healing into the workplace. It is time for us to exercise a conscious choice, and to act from our integrity and what we know is right about how to treat people in the workplace.

Let's go to work!"[33]

As we face tomorrow, we must all come to realize that only we can help ourselves. No longer will the big company rescue us, or provide a safe haven for an extended period. We are not alone.

Millions of people throughout the country are facing the same changes. We are searching for answers and productive ways to fit within the American Business community.

We can choose to change how we go to work, how we work together, and how we learn, and how we approach risk. We can choose self-reliance, collaboration, continuous learning, and independence. Added to these choices, streamlining of Corporate America, combined with new supply and demand of the Information Age and global markets, mean greater opportunity than ever for The Entrepreneurial Class.

VIII.
Rules of the Game

What advice do we have for companies, for individuals, and for both?

ADVICE FOR COMPANIES

Talk to your people. Help them to figure out what they want, and what you want. Be honest with each other, and do not be afraid of the 'tough' conversations, when expectations and performance do not match up.

Build development plans for everyone. Make this task part of the compensation structure of every manager and team member in the corporation. Penalize people who ignore the process, and reward those who excel at using development plans to identify and grow individuals.

Know what your company does well, and how your people contribute to that success. Know where your company fails, or does poorly. Face this honestly. Discuss it openly, and ask every employee to participate in the solutions. To the extent that shortcomings result from lack of development plans and inability to predict and appropriately fill resource needs, change and change quickly.

Let people know where they stand. If it is on shaky ground, state the facts. Identify the extent to which the shaky ground results from poor or inappropriate performance, and where skills may not match corporate needs.

Know the value of experience, as it relates to each job. Let employees be aware of the value the corporation places on experience, and how that may vary from job-to-job or area-to-area. Help employees decide how they can use their experience to their advantage, either within the corporation or in the marketplace.

Do not be afraid to 'lose' people, since you are going to lose them anyway. Do be afraid of losing people for the wrong reasons. Do be afraid of keeping people for the wrong reasons. Help to avoid traps of keeping and losing the wrong people by communicating widely and with clarity things like: where the corporation is going, what jobs the corporation will need and not need in 1, 3 and 5 years. Make training available to help employees change skills, particularly when their jobs may not be needed on the 1-5 year horizon.

Value people. Know that they like to contribute, and most often will, if they understand the rules of the game, and if they have the right equipment with which to play. Also, know that if they do not like the game, they will most likely move on to another field eventually. If you can help them move on, you and they will probably respect each other, and may do each other some good sometime in the future.

Never forget that the game goes on and on, at least until we die or retire. Just as one good turn deserves another, so does one bad turn. Treat an employee unfairly, and they will most likely remember for a lifetime. Use an employee poorly to achieve some short term goal, and you may see the company make some short term gain. However, remember the payback could be a bitch—and the company will never be in control of the payback timing.

Never underestimate the ability of an individual to excel, whether with your company or with someone else.

If an individual contributes today, and fails tomorrow, look to the job and the clarity of success and failure definitions. The employee either did not understand the rules, thought she was playing some other game, or was overwhelmed.

Remember, teach and reward the principle that failure at a task does not equal failure as a person. And, remember that when meeting with an employee to review under-performance.

As a manager, ask yourself this:
- Have I made it clear what is expected?
- Are my expectations task specific, and carefully defined?
- Am I willing to tell it like it is?
- Do I give co-workers, subordinates and team members opportunity, direction, and support?

If not, why not?

Do not forget to celebrate the successes, and learn from the failures.

But never forget that most people learn more from crises and challenges than they do when things go well.

ADVICE FOR INDIVIDUALS AND COMPANIES

Know your value-add. If you don't know it, figure it out, and quickly. Write it down. Figure out how to expand on it. Compare how it matches to what you hear employers, team members and customers say they need.

Acknowledging failure in today's environment of continuous improvement is a given. Celebrating success can be much more rare. Don't forget to recognize the progress you and those around you are making. Be quick to congratulate yourself and others for work well done.

Learn as much as you can as fast as you can.

Embrace change. If change is scary recognize you are not alone, but get used to it. Change is inevitable, and you might as well be a part of it, rather than following in the undertow, out of control.

Figure out what you are doing about diversity in your life. Figure out what else you are going to do about it. Get comfortable with diversity. Get to know people who are not at all like yourself. Find out how they are different. Figure out how diversity can make you richer, more interesting.

Jobs and growth, like life, are a path and a process, not an end.

When one door closes, another opens.

For those who ask if things at work can ever get better—they can, for those who are willing to make changes happen.

Figure out exactly where you are financially. How much do you owe? How quickly could you pay it off if you had to? How long could you delay any payments if you had to? How many weeks, or months, of income do you have saved? How are you going to increase savings, starting now?

Use adversity to your advantage, until it turns to good.

ADVICE FOR INDIVIDUALS

Figure out what you want from your relationship with a company. Write it down. File the list away where you can find it again. When an offer comes along, write down the attributes of the offer and the company. Then, pull the old list out and compare. Do they match? If they don't, figure out why not.

Don't let money be the only determinant when making job decisions. In the long run the other factors can far outweigh any short term financial gain. Happiness, having opportunities to get ahead, working in a learning environment, having respect for peers, managers and company, all make life worth living.

Know where you are going. Write it down. If you don't know, that's okay, too. But work on figuring it out.

Look at building intelligence as another form of exercise. Just as exercising the body builds physical muscle, exercising the brain builds intellectual muscle.

Arrogance gets more people into trouble more often than just about any other behavior.

Never think you are untouchable. Never think you are smarter than everyone else, or that you know better.

Success can be fleeting. Keep after it.

Do not wait for the corporation to approach you. Ask for advice, insist on your right to feedback, and be open to negatives and positives. Remember, the positives are nice to hear, the negatives are probably the greatest opportunities to learn and grow.

Develop your own plan of where you want to go. Know what milestones you want to achieve, and what steps you have to take to get there. Know what you want and are willing to give up to get there.

Write out your own statement of goals and values. Write down the tradeoffs you are willing to make to achieve them. Put it away for a while and then revisit it from time to time. Update it along the way. Take time to reflect on how it may change over time, and on how the changes affect your ability to perform at work.

Ask for facts. Be wary when facts are unavailable, especially when it comes to defining job performance. Do not be afraid to take risks, or operate in undefined territory. Do at least get some tangible success measures, or be willing to risk getting sand-bagged along the way.

Do not mistake calculated risk taking with operating without a safety net. Practice can never make perfect. Be aware that bad things sometimes happen to good people. When they do, be prepared to move on, while learning from the situation.

Know what you are worth, and ask others to provide feedback on their perception of the same. If their perceptions do not match your reality, it may be time for a reality check, or a new environment. Know the difference between the two. 'Reality check' means realigning your skills to meet job and task opportunities. 'Moving on' means finding a new working environment, with new rules about how employee and company deal with each other.

When preparing to move on, ask lots of questions of potential new employers. Ask how they measure, define and reward performance. Ask how they plan to help you grow. Ask for examples of how they have done this for others in the past. If examples are scarce, beware.

When trying to decide whether to move on, or stay, be aware that things tend to look greener elsewhere. Make your evaluation as fact-based as possible, to get beyond the rose-colored-glass syndrome.

List what you want. Talk to the company about that list. Do not be afraid of the conversation. If they cannot supply your needs, better you should know that now than waste precious years chasing an illusion. Who knows, you may find out they can meet your needs, and just did not know what they were.

Figure out your retirement needs. How many years of retirement have you saved away? When do you want to retire—or at least quit your day job? How many years after that do you expect to live? How much money will you need to live on in each year of your retirement?

Get advice from a financial planner. In the meantime, try this quick and dirty set of calculations. Multiply together the number of years you expect to live in retirement and the amount you think you will need in each year of your retirement. Subtract the amount of money you have already saved for retirement. Divide by the number of years between now and the year you want to retire. That is the amount you have to earn each year, including interest, to meet your financial retirement dreams. Can you save that amount each year? If not, it is time to figure out a new strategy—quickly!

If you lost your job tomorrow, what would you do? How would you pay for it? Figure it out! Then act on it! Someday you will probably lose your job. You might as well be prepared, or, even better, act preemptively.

IX.
Epilogue
Sarah Doesn't Work Here Anymore

Sarah was downsized in 1988, and then again nearly eight years later. Her story is about these two very different experiences—the first she lived through with fear and panic, the second she approached with confidence and optimism. This is the story of what happened to Sarah, and of how Sarah's approach had changed, making the two experiences so different.

ROUND ONE—TERROR

By 1988, Sarah had worked for nearly 10 years in a large, well known financial institution, holding a number of responsible positions, in different divisions of the company. This is what she told us about the first downsizing.

> This company was my third employer in my business career. I had experience in customer service, sales, strategic planning and new product development. I viewed myself as very successful and capable, and thrilled at the challenges I encountered each day at work. I liked most of my co-workers and believed in what we were doing.
>
> In 1988, I felt as if I had everything going for me—a great company, good jobs with new opportunities, expanded responsibilities every two to three years, a wonderfully supportive spouse who was a practicing lawyer also making a good income, a bright, beautiful one year old child, a lovely home, a nanny, ski trips in the winter, vacations at the beach in the summer—you get the picture.

I had spent the previous two years on a development project. They recruited me to join this project as they were moving it out of strategic planning and assigning it to a Business Unit. Then, in 1988, this project was shut down because the head of the Business Unit did not believe it fit with the overall goals and objectives.

On a Thursday afternoon, the head of our group and our senior human resources officer met with me. They told me that I was to be offered a severance package. I knew it was coming, and still I was devastated. They said that no other jobs were available at my level in this Business Unit; they were not sure what might be available in the other Business Units. They assured me that I was good and something would come along. I was told I was free to pursue any opportunities inside or outside the company, and received a good recommendation and some outplacement assistance to help with the job search.

The next couple of weeks were spent in a flurry of activity, meeting with members of my staff who were also out of jobs. We wound down activity, closed the operation. Then I went home and started a job hunt campaign which lasted six months before I found another job.

Those six months in 1988 were some of the longest and toughest days of my life. There were no job offers during that period. Friends were sympathetic, but not very helpful. I networked my brains out, and it seemed to get me nowhere. This had never happened before; I had never had trouble finding a job before.

One afternoon I took a long walk, and played out in my mind, 'What's the worst that can happen if I don't find a job?' I thought, 'We could lose the house, be in debt up to our eyeballs, have to turn to welfare . . .' I kept telling myself, 'No matter what, I

won't be dead. We can recover from anything else.'
It didn't help. I was so scared.[1]

ROUND TWO—CONFIDENCE

Well, eventually I found a good job, and an
even better one after that. Now, again, the company I
work for is downsizing, and I am a valuable, albeit
expensive, member of the management team. This
time I look forward to leaving, even though I will go
with less severance and more debt than I had in
1988.[2]

What is the difference between 1988 and 1995, we
wondered? Sarah shared her thoughts.

In 1988, I defined myself by my job title. I was
a Vice President in a well known financial
institution. I saw myself as a worker in the corporate
world. When I lost my job, I could not conceive of
doing anything other than becoming an employee in
another company.

I felt powerless. Potential employers were in
control of when, or if, I would get to interview for a
position. No matter how good my skills, if the guy on
the other side of the interview table did not see a fit,
I was out.

I believed I needed permanent, full time work
in order to be rewarded, financially and
professionally. I could not imagine successfully
working on my own. Every time I thought of being
an independent contractor, I saw pictures of my
waitressing days from high school and college.[3]

That was 1988. What has changed now? Sarah continued.

Now, I don't know if I will ever work
permanently for a company again. I define myself by

> the things I know I am good at, like sales, customer
> service, building businesses.
>   I am building a business practice of my own.
> By selling my time and effort in small chunks, I
> work as a consultant to businesses who need my
> skills but cannot afford me full time. I still call on
> companies, but instead of pursuing a full time job, I
> look for project work.[4]

We describe the importance of 'role identity' in the Chapter,
The Entrepreneurial Class, under, 'redefining self and work.' By
the second downsizing, Sarah had changed the way she identified
herself and her relationship to work. As part of the transition to
The Entrepreneurial Class, Sarah had come to see herself as
separate from her title, her company, her perks. We expect she
will continue to work on her definition of herself socially in
relation to the work she is doing. However, she has passed the
greatest hurdle to entering The Entrepreneurial Class. She is
willing to let the work and the projects, not the title and the
company, help to define who she is and what she does.

Sarah described one other important change she had made
between her first and second downsizing experiences.

> After 1988, I enrolled in an MBA program to
> update my skills and add to my credentials. I worked
> full time while I went to school, and it was hard.
> However, now I have something additional the
> marketplace values.[5]

Sarah was willing to go back to school, to learn, to enhance
existing skills and to build new skills. In addition, when she went
back to school, she knew for what purpose she was going. We
have observed that many people, women in particular, will
assume that they are not getting ahead because they lack
education or technical expertise in a particular area. They then set
off to pursue education, in hopes that it will lead to something. In
Sarah's case however, she appropriately positioned education as

an addition to what she already knew she wanted to do. She used education to complement and round out her existing skills.

RE-DEFINING SELF AND WORK

Finally, Sarah talked about her vision for the future.

> I still expect to sometimes have dry spells between jobs. Nevertheless, never again will I give away to some employer the perception of power over my destiny. Nor will I give away the right to define who I am as a professional. I know what I am good at, I know a market exists for what I can do. Between jobs, I do what I want to do.[6]

Sarah kept emphasizing that the major difference was in the way she saw herself professionally.

> "Contemporary society is built on a social system in which the individual's livelihood, place, worth, and sense of self are increasingly defined by his or her job. At the same time jobs are disappearing.
> ". . .Yet there is a colossal amount of things waiting to be done—building decent places to live, exploring the universe, making cities less dangerous places, teaching one another, helping to raise our children, visiting, comforting, healing, feeding one another, dancing, making music, telling stories, inventing things, and governing ourselves. But much of the essential activity people have always undertaken to raise and to educate their families, to enjoy themselves, to give pleasure to others, and to promote the general welfare is not considered work and is not packaged as a job."[7]

WOMEN'S WORK

Whatever the reasons, women are leaving their employers in large numbers. They are taking years of experience and hard earned skills with them. They are also doing so at a time in which changes due to the Information Age may favor their success in high measure.

> "For female executives, there is no convention. Just as they made their own way into the corporate suites, they are now making their own way out—and confounding the companies that had been grooming them for years. So many women have started their own firms that as a group they now employ about three-quarters as many workers in the U.S. as the Fortune 500."[8]

Many women seem to be striking out to integrate personal style, ideals and personal vision with work life. They seem, whether consciously or not, to be pursuing a more holistic approach, using the skills they have built in Corporate America to build businesses. In interviews, they frequently bring up the word, 'values.' It is as if their inner voice is different from that of many of their male counterparts, reminding them of another way to live one's work life—pursuing something other than financial rewards and affiliation. Need for affiliation and membership seem to play less of a role for women. They seem more willing to move on and create their own team, where they can practice a leadership and management style in keeping with their personal goals and values.

Expectations And Reality

The push into management positions in the workforce during the 1970s, observes one editor,

> ". . . may have unrealistically raised expectations of the role work and career could play

in the lives of women, especially as the climb got steeper, the pyramid grew narrower, and the thrill of the chase faded away."[9]

Women are experiencing

- a sense of power about what they've already accomplished;
- a sense of freedom from having proved themselves over and over; and
- increasing restlessness at having to play the game by the old male rules.[10]

Many women who entered business in the 1970s have spent little time plotting the strategy of their careers, or examining the choices they made. In the 1970s, as women broke into Corporate America in large numbers, they took whatever opportunities were available. Unlike their white male counterparts, who assumed they would be welcome at whatever they chose to do, women entered big business where they could, followed opportunities as they presented themselves, and carved their own paths without the advantage, advice, or roadmap of a preceding generation. Now, they are opting out of the game of big business in greater numbers than their male counterparts.

> "One reason some women weary of the game is the haphazard way they've played it. They took random walks down their career paths, following the advice of mentors rather than playing to their own strengths; taking whatever came along without necessarily taking stock of themselves. Some have reached midlife only to find they've been on the wrong path."[11]

Now that they have broken in and established themselves in business, many more opportunities are open to women to pursue their dreams, inside and outside of the large corporate arena. As a consequence, they are following the process that has contributed to their success all along—random walks—even as they opt to

proceed with work and career in more independent environments.
Author Sally Helgesen refers to this more random approach as
'The Strategy of the Web'[12].

> ". . . women were supposed to be hampered by
> a more diffuse, less goal-oriented notion of their
> careers: by tending to see their work 'as personal
> growth, as self-fulfillment, as satisfaction, as making
> a contribution to others, as doing *what one wants to
> do*. The difference (in defining career progress of
> men vs. women), then, came down to a question of
> *strategy*: men had a definite, objective plan for
> getting to where they wanted, while women, as a
> general rule, lacked such a plan . . .
>
> "This   (assumption   of   a   hierarchical,
> manipulative, win-lose, chain-of-command) is surely
> how strategy is generally perceived, but it need not
> be the only way. The strategy of the web employs
> different methods in order to achieve different goals .
> . .
>
> "The strategy of the web is less direct, less
> focused on specific goals, . . . it works in a less linear
> fashion than hierarchical strategies.
>
> ". . . The strategy of the web is guided by
> opportunity, proceeds by the use of intuition, and is
> characterized by a patience that comes of wanting to
> see what comes next.
>
> ". . . In mythologies all over the world, female
> deities are depicted at the loom, knitting together the
> fabric of human life, spinning out the thread that
> links the events of the past with the potentialities—
> the unborn people and events—of the future . . .
>
> "For this reason, the spinning goddesses of
> Germanic and Greek myth were also the goddesses
> of fate. Their recognition and acceptance of destiny
> as the interweave of past and future, of chance and
> work, is the ultimate expression of the strategy of the
> web. And at the most profound level, this is what . . .
> (women) echo when they describe themselves as
> trusting that the opportunities which come their way

will unlock their futures. Like the ancient female
goddesses, they understand that the future cannot be
reduced to a simple matter of objectives, nor be
achieved by the mere application of will.[13]

These deviations from traditional, and therefore primarily
male, models of career development were echoed by women we
interviewed, and came up repeatedly in our reading. Women
talked about their careers in terms of random walks, search for
inclusion, desire to move beyond hierarchy, willingness to trust.
These sentiments were expressed by a woman who had recently
left a company at the top of the Forbes 500 to form her own
company.

When I and my friends started out in the late
1970s, it seemed exciting to say that we were
interviewing at the cream of the Forbes and Fortune
50—places where few women had gone before.
Having a business card with the name of a major
firm seemed to mean clout. Our male role models
kept telling us that clout was good, that we needed
power if we were going to succeed.

With few female role models to tell us
otherwise, we bought in. We pursued the brass ring
of big titles, big perks, big salaries. The price was
conformity, to a set of rules with which we could not
identify—because our fathers and brothers wrote
them. These rules did not account for our differences
in speech, style of presentation, need for
collaboration.

So, now, we opt out, and use the traits that led
to our success in the companies we worked for, to
build new success models. Listening, seeking
opinions, admitting vulnerability, collaborating,
taking risks, being willing to work long hours, desire
for near-perfection, joy in achieving success, these
are all things that contribute to our success in our
new ventures.

We are also very conscious of the two sides to ourselves—the creative side and the numbers side, I call them—and the need to build balance between them. So often jobs I have had have emphasized the numbers side. They left me with little opportunity to express myself, which is where I feel I make a real contribution to the world. Many of my male friends scoff when I say that, but my female friends understand.[14]

Differences In Approach

Women seem less constrained than their male counterparts by a need to achieve gratification by staying within the confines of major companies. They seem more willing to take the risks and strike out on their own—albeit often after much reflection, with a well-thought-out plan and the cushion of a severance package, negotiated in thanks for work well done. Often, they also have the support of working spouses who can cushion the blow of walking away from high five and six figure incomes.

"When a full-fledged midlife crisis comes along, though, nearly all (of a group of men interviewed for the article) agreed that a woman is likely to handle it much better than a man."[15]

According to a manager at a New York financial institution,
". . . women who are encouraged to face their failures usually bounce back better than men. 'Women excessively blame themselves, so there's always a danger that failure will make them too cautious, even paranoid, about risk taking. But women are taught that it's okay to ask for help, so they respond better to feedback. Women learn faster. Men deflect mistakes. Men are taught, of course, never to show any weakness.'[16]

No Time For Politics

> ". . . it was women, more often than men, who seemed to feel that all that was necessary for success was to do a great job, that superior performance would be recognized and rewarded. Yet looking around, I could see that much more seemed to go into getting recognized and rewarded, and I saw men much more often than women behaving in these ways.
>
> "In addition to doing excellent work, you must make sure that your work is recognized. This may consist of making a point to tell your boss, or your boss's boss what you have done . . . When lunchtime comes, the one who eats lunch with the boss may be doing more to get ahead than the one who stays in the office, eating a sandwich and working."[17]

Sarah commented on her motivation for changing, moving out of a large company environment in which she had obviously been successful for many years.

> I just don't want to play the games anymore. It just doesn't fit anymore. I no longer want to be a part of winning, at the expense of someone else losing; caring more about myself than I do about my team; serving up numbers and reports I don't believe in to make someone higher up look good. I no longer want to fight with other departments' competing agendas to get the company to move forward.
>
> I want to be able to work collaboratively. I want to do good work, know that it is good, enjoy my customers, meet their needs simply and effectively, and go home to enjoy my family. I want to reduce report writing and maximize output. I want to continue to learn—be a real renaissance person— and then put that knowledge to work for the betterment of myself and those around me. I want to lead and facilitate change in a way that is productive.

Companies and individuals can do better, and I want
to be there to help make it happen—I just don't want
it to own me. I prize my freedom, and I hope I can
sustain my choice to operate independently in
Corporate America.

I do believe a better way to live and to work is
possible, and I want to find it. Maybe it's like
searching for utopia, but I have to look.[18]

To Sarah, and all of those like her, who have gone on to find
another way, good luck! May their successes fuel the dreams of
all the others still to come.

Endnotes

Chapter One
Where Are We Going?

[1] Tomasko, Robert M. *Rethinking the Corporation: The Architecture of Change.* New York, N.Y.: AMACOM, 1993, p. 70

[2] Imparato, Nicholas and Harari, Oren. When New Worlds Stir. *Management Review*, October, 1994, p. 22-28.

[3] Imparato, Nicholas and Harari, Oren. *Jumping the Curve: Innovation and Strategic Choice in an Age of Transition.* San Francisco, Ca.: Jossey-Bass Publishers, 1994.

Chapter Two
Historical Perspective

[1] Imparato, Nicholas and Harari, Oren. *Jumping the Curve: Innovation and Strategic Choice in an Age of Transition.* San Francisco, Ca.: Jossey-Bass Publishers, 1994, p. 30.

[2] Ramirez, Anthony. AT&T Offer: One Said No, One Said Yes: Buyout Decisions By 2 of the 72,000. *The New York Times*: Dec. 10, 1995, p. 3.1, 3.11.

[3] Barnet, Richard J. and Cavanagh, John. *Global Dreams, Imperial Corporations and the New World Order.* New York, N.Y.: Simon & Schuster, 1994, p. 312-313.

[4] Interview, Philadelphia, 1991

[5] National Small Business United and Arthur Andersen Enterprise Group. *Survey of Small and Mid-Sized Businesses Trends for 1995.* National Small Business United (NSBU): 1155 15th Street, N.W., Suite 710; Washington, D.C. 20005; 202-293-8830, p. 23.

[6] Ramirez, AT&T Offer.

[7] Ramirez, Anthony. Take the Money and Walk? How to Decide. *The New York Times*: Dec. 10, 1995, p. 3.11.

[8] Baxandall, Rosalyn and Gordon, Linda. *America's Working Women: A Documentary History, 1600 to the present.* New York, N.Y.: W. W. Norton & Company, 1995, p. 289-290.

[9] Bruchey, Stuart. Enterprise*: The Dynamic Economy of a Free People.* Cambridge, Ma.: Harvard University Press, 1990, p. 533.

[10] Case, John. A Company of Business People. *INC*: April, 1993, 79-93.

[11] Imparato, Nicholas and Harari, Oren. *Jumping the Curve*, p. 72.

[12] Bruchey, Stuart. Enterprise, p.523-526.

[13] Imparato, Nicholas and Harari, Oren. *Jumping the Curve*, p. 32.

[14] Bruchey, Stuart. *Enterprise*, p 526.

[15] Barnet, Richard J. and Cavanagh, John. *Global Dreams*, p. 426.

[16] Imparato, Nicholas and Harari, Oren. *Jumping the Curve*, p. 185.

[17] Bruchey, Stuart. *Enterprise*, p. 512.

[18] Barnet, Richard J. and Cavanagh, John. *Global Dreams*, p. 425.

[19] Imparato, Nicholas and Harari, Oren. *Jumping the Curve*, p. 48.

Chapter Three
Corporate America Is Changing

[1] Ramirez, Anthony. AT&T Offer: One Said No, One Said Yes: Buyout Decisions By 2 of the 72,000. *The New York Times*: Dec. 10, 1995, p. 3.1, 3.11.

[2] Imparato, Nicholas and Harari, Oren. *Jumping the Curve: Innovation and Strategic Choice in an Age of Transition.* San Francisco, Ca.: Jossey-Bass Publishers, 1994, p. 188-192.

[3] Thompson, John A. with Henningsen, Catherine A. *The Portable Executive.* New York, N.Y.: Simon & Schuster, 1995, p. 14.

[4] Tomasko, Robert M. *Rethinking the Corporation: The Architecture of Change.* New York, N.Y.: AMACOM, 1993, p. 2-3.

[5] Stewart, Thomas A. Which Side Are You On? The Never-Ending War For A Manager's Soul. *Fortune Magazine*: May 15, 1995, p. 12, 124.

[6] IBID, p. 12.

[7] Imparato, Nicholas and Harari, Oren. *Jumping the Curve*, p 55.

[8] Case, John. A Company of Business People. *INC*: April, 1993, p. 80.

[9] Stewart, Thomas A. Which Side Are You On?, p. 12.

[10] Jaffe, Denis T. and Scott, Cynthia D. and Tobe, Glenn R. *Rekindling Commitment: How to Revitalize Yourself, Your Work, and Your Organization.* San Francisco, Ca. Jossey-Bass Publishers, 1994, p. 52-53.

[11] Harari, Oren. Open the Doors, Tell the Truth. *Management Review:* Jan., 1995, p. 33-35.

[12] Jaffe, Denis T. and Scott, Cynthia D. and Tobe, Glenn R. *Rekindling Commitment*, p. 11-12.

[13] Tomasko, Robert M. *Rethinking the Corporation*, p. 52-53.

[14] Hequet, Marc. Flat and Happy? *Training:* April, 1995. P. 29-34.

[15] Tomasko, Robert M. *Rethinking the Corporation,* p. 96.

[16] Labich, Kenneth. Kissing Off. *Fortune Magazine:* February 20, 1995, p. 44.

[17] IBID, p. 44.

[18] Imparato, Nicholas and Harari, Oren. When New Worlds Stir. *Management Review*, October, 1994, p. 22-28.

[19] Bruchey, Stuart. *Enterprise: The Dynamic Economy of a Free People.* Cambridge, Ma.: Harvard University Press, 1990, p. 533.

[20] Filipczak, Bob. You're On Your Own. *Training:* Jan, 1995, p.29-36.

[21] Imparato, Nicholas and Harari, Oren. When New Worlds Stir, p. 22-28.

[22] Bartlett, Christopher A. and Ghoshal, Sumantra. Matrix Management: Not A Structure, A Frame of Mind. *Harvard Business Review:* July-August, 1990, p. 142.

[23] McKesson, Mike. GM President to Take Wheel as Chairman. *Gannett Suburban Newspapers:* December 5, 1995, p. 5B.

[24] Bartlett, Christopher A. and Ghoshal, Sumantra. Matrix Management, p. 139.

[25] Newman, William H., Editor. *Manager for the Year 2000.* Englewood, N.J.: Prentice Hall, Inc., 1978, p. 41.

[26] Imparato, Nicholas and Harari, Oren. *Jumping the Curve: Innovation and Strategic Choice in an Age of Transition.* San Francisco, Ca.: Jossey-Bass Publishers, 1994, p. 73.

[27] Newman, William H., Editor. *Manager for the Year 2000*, p.43-44.

[28] IBID, p. 103.

[29] Morin, William J. *Silent Sabotage: Rescuing Our Careers, Our Companies and Our Lives From the Creeping Paralysis of Anger and Bitterness.* New York, N.Y.: AMACOM, 1995, p. 149-152.

[30] Interview, New York, 1993.
[31] Filipczak, Bob.You're On Your Own. *Training*: Jan.,1995, p. 29-36.
[32] Interview, Connecticut, 1993.
[33] IBID.
[34] IBID.
[35] IBID.
[36] Jaffe, Denis T. and Scott, Cynthia D. and Tobe, Glenn R. *Rekindling Commitment*, p. 199.
[37] IBID, p. 200.
[38] Tomasko, Robert M. *Rethinking the Corporation*, p. 169.
[39] Imparato, Nicholas and Harari, Oren. *Jumping the Curve*, P. 72-74.
[40] Thompson, John. A. with Henningsen, Catherine A. *The Portable Executive*, P. 28.
[41] Labich, Kenneth. Kissing Off, p. 44-51.

Chapter Four
Diversity

[1] Thomas, R. Roosevelt, Jr. From Affirmative Action to Affirming Diversity. *Harvard Business Review*: March-April, 1990, p. 115.
[2] Tannen, Deborah. *Talking From 9 To 5: How Women's and Men's Conversational Styles Affect Who Gets Heard, Who Gets Credit, and What Gets Done At Work*. New York, N.Y.: William Morrow and Company, Inc., 1994, p. 169.
[3] Imparato, Nicholas and Harari, Oren. *Jumping the Curve: Innovation and Strategic Choice in an Age of Transition*. San Francisco, Ca.: Jossey-Bass Publishers, 1994, p. 187.
[4] Thomas, R. Roosevelt, Jr. From Affirmative Action to Affirming Diversity, 107-117.
[5] Cox, Taylor H. and Blake, Stacy. Managing Cultural Diversity: Implications for Organizational Competitiveness. *Academy of Management Executive*, 1991, Vol. 5, No. 3, p. 45-56.
[6] McCoy, Frank. Shattering Glass Ceilings. *Black Enterprise*: Sept., 1985, p. 22.
[7] Edmond, Alfred, Jr. The BE 100's: Evolution/Revolution. *Black Enterprise*: June, 1995, p. 86.

[8] Barnet, Richard J. and Cavanagh, John. *Global Dreams, Imperial Corporations and the New World Order*. New York, N.Y.: Simon & Schuster, 1994, p. 298-299.

[9] Bruchey, Stuart. *Enterprise: The Dynamic Economy of a Free People*. Cambridge, Ma.: Harvard University Press, 1990. p. 534.

[10] Morris, Betsy. Executive Women Confront Midlife Crisis. *Fortune Magazine*, September 18, 1995, p. 65.

[11] IBID, p. 74.

[12] Tannen, Deborah. *Talking From 9 To 5*, p. 130.

[13] McCoy, Frank. Shattering Glass Ceilings, p. 22.

[14] Bruchey, Stuart. *Enterprise*, p.536.

[15] Sabir, Nadirah Z. Moving On Up.*Black Enterprise*.Sept.,1995,p. 26.

[16] IBID, p. 26.

[17] Edmond, Alfred, Jr. The BE 100's, p. 96.

[18] Brown, Carolyn M. All Talk, No Action. *Black Enterprise*: Sept., 1995, p. 63.

[19] IBID, p. 63.

[20] IBID, p. 62.

[21] IBID, p. 62.

[22] IBID, p. 64.

[23] Imparato, Nicholas and Harari, Oren. *Jumping the Curve*, p. 188

[24] Hayes, Cassandra. The New Spin On Corporate Work Teams. *Black Enterprise*: June, 1995, p. 229.

[25] Tannen, Deborah. *Talking From 9 To* 5, p. 200.

[26] Hayes, Cassandra. The New Spin On Corporate Work Teams, p. 230-231.

[27] Morris, Betsy. Executive Women Confront Midlife Crisis, p. 60.

[28] IBID, p. 62.

[29] Interview, New England, 1993

[30] IBID

[31] IBID

[32] IBID

[33] Interview, Midwest, 1994

[34] Morris, Betsy. Executive Women Confront Midlife Crisis, p. 55.

[35] IBID, p. 55.

[36] IBID, p. 74.

[37] IBID, p. 74-78.

[38] Tannen, Deborah. *Talking From 9 To 5*, p.60.

[39] IBID, p. 236.

[40] IBID, p. 236.

[41] IBID, p. 36.

[42] IBID, p.40-41.

[43] Labich, Kenneth. Kissing Off. *Fortune Magazine*: February 20, 1995, p. 50.

[44] Hay, Louise L. *Heal Your Body*. Carson, Ca.: Hay House, Inc., 1994, p. 27.

[45] Cox, Taylor H. & Blake, Stacy. Managing Cultural Diversity, p. 48.

[46] Interview, Midwest, 1994.

[47] Van Eron, Ann M., Ways To Assess Diversity Success. *HR Magazine*, Aug., 1995, P. 51-52.

[48] Tannen, Deborah. *Talking From 9 To 5*, p. 203.

[49] Van Eron, Ann M., Ways To Assess Diversity Success.

[50] Tannen, Deborah. *Talking From 9 To 5*, p. 52

[51] Cox, Taylor H. and Blake, Stacy. Managing Cultural Diversity.

[52] IBID.

[53] Moss-Kanter, Rosabeth. *The Change Masters*. New York, N.Y.: Simon & Schuster, 1993.

[54] Levering, Robert and Moskowitz, Milton. *The 100 Best Companies to Work for in America*. New York, N.Y.: Penguin Books USA Inc., 1994.

[55] Interview at Xerox Headquarters, Stamford, Connecticut, 1993

[56] Thomas, R. Roosevelt, Jr. From Affirmative Action to Affirming Diversity, p. 115.

Chapter Five
Company Success

[1] Interview, New England, 1993

[2] IBID, p. 53.

[3] Sellers, Patricia. Now Bounce Back! *Fortune Magazine*: May 1, 1995, p. 49-66.

[4] Morin, William J. Silent Sabotage: *Rescuing Our Careers, Our Companies and Our Lives From the Creeping Paralysis of Anger and Bitterness*. New York, N.Y.: AMACOM, 1995, p. 55-56.

[5] Interview, New York, 1995

[6] Interview, Midwest, 1995
[7] Hequet, Marc. Flat and Happy? *Training*: April, 1995. P. 29-34.
[8] IBID
[9] IBID
[10] IBID
[11] Tomasko, Robert M. *Rethinking the Corporation*, p. 165.
[12] IBID, p. 168.
[13] Interview, Northeast, 1993
[14] Interview, Southeast, 1993.
[15] Interview, Northeast, 1993

Chapter Six
Promotions

[1] Interview, Northeast, 1993
[2] Interview, Midwest, 1995
[3] IBID
[4] IBID
[5] Interview, New York, 1993
[6] Brown, Thomas. Defining a 'New Social Contract.' *Industry Week*: Aug. 15, 1994, p. 52.
[7] Filipczak, Bob.You're On Your Own. *Training*: Jan., 1995, p. 29-36.

Chapter Seven
The Entrepreneurial Class

[1] Predictions: Slower Economic Growth Will Leave Many Behind. *U.S. News & World Report*. Dec. 25, 1995, p. 81.
[2] IBID, p. 82.
[3] Interview, Northeast, 1995
[4] WFAS News Broadcast. Dec. 18, 1995. Quoted New York's 89th District Representative Naomi Matusov.

[5] Nat'l Small Business United & Arthur Andersen Enterprise Group. *Survey of Small and Mid-Sized Businesses: Trends for 1995*, p. 1.

[6] IBID.

[7] IBID, p. 13.

[8] IBID, p. 13.

[9] IBID, P 14.

[10] Driscoll, Dawn-Marie and Goldberg, Carol. *Members of the Club: The Coming of Age of Executive Women*. New York, N.Y.: The Free Press, 1993, p. 71.

[11] Predictions. The Beat Goes Online: Bill Gates. *U.S. News & World Report*. Dec. 25, 1995, p. 82.

[12] Filipczak, Bob. You're On Your Own. *Training*: Jan.,1995, p. 29-36.

[13] Nat'l Small Business United & Arthur Andersen Enterprise Group. *Survey of Small and Mid-Sized Businesses*, p. 21.

[14] IBID, p. 16-17.

[15] IBID, p. 6.

[16] IBID, p. 9.

[17] Interview, Northeast, 1995

[18] Selz, Michael. Costs of Complying With Federal Rules Weigh More Heavily on Small Firms. *Wall Street Journal*: October 1, 1995.

[19] Nat'l Small Business United & Arthur Andersen Enterprise Group. *Survey of Small and Mid-Sized Businesses*, p. 8.

[20] Interview, Northeast, 1995

[21] Schine, Eric. Benefits are Being Pecked to Death. *Business Week*: Dec. 4, 1995, p. 42.

[22] Nat'l Small Business United & Arthur Andersen Enterprise Group. *Survey of Small and Mid-Sized Businesses*, p.32.

[23] IBID, p. 26.

[24] IBID, p. 18.

[25] IBID, p. 18.

[26] National Small Business United. *Issue Briefs. For Delegates To the 1995 White House Conference On Small Business*, June 11-15, 1995, p. 5.

[27] IBID, p. 5.

[28] Filipczak, Bob. You're On Your Own. *Training*: Jan.,1995.

[29] Thompson, John A. with Henningsen, Catherine A. *The Portable Executive*. New York, N.Y.: Simon & Schuster, 1995, p. 10-11.

[30] IBID, p. 11.

[31] IBID, p. 147.

[32] IBID, p. 99.

[33] Marshall, Edward M. *Transforming the Way We Work: The Power of the Collaborative Workplace*. New York, N.Y.: AMACOM, 1995, p. 181.

Chapter Eight
The Rules Of The Game

No Citations

Chapter Nine
Sarah Doesn't Work Here Anymore

[1] Interview, Northeast, 1995.

[2] IBID

[3] IBID

[4] IBID

[5] IBID

[6] IBID

[7] Barnet, Richard J. and Cavanagh, John. *Global Dreams, Imperial Corporations and the New World Order*. New York, N.Y.: Simon & Schuster, 1994, p. 426-427.

[8] Morris, Betsy. Executive Women Confront Midlife Crisis. *Fortune Magazine*, September 18, 1995, p. 68.

[9] IBID, p. 65.

[10] IBID, p. 68.

[11] IBID, p. 78-80.

[12] Driscoll, Dawn-Marie and Goldberg, Carol. *Members of the Club: The Coming of Age of Executive Women*. New York, N.Y.: The Free Press, 1993, p. 248.

[13] Helgesen, Sally. *The Female Advantage*. New York, N.Y.: Doubleday, 1990, p. 57-60.

[14] Interview, Northeast, 1995

[15] Morris, Betsy. Executive Women Confront Midlife Crisis, p. 72.

[16] Sellers, Patricia. Now Bounce Back! *Fortune Magazine*: May 1, 1995, p. 64-66.

[17] Tannen, Deborah. *Talking From 9 To 5: How Women's and Men's Conversational Styles Affect Who Gets Heard, Who Gets Credit, and What Gets Done At Work.* New York, N.Y.: William Morrow and Company, Inc., 1994, P 135.

[18] Interview, Northeast, 1995.

Bibliography

Aburdene, Patricia & Naisbitt, John. *Megatrends for Women*. New York, N.Y.: Villard Books, 1992.

Aley, James. Where The Jobs Are. *Fortune Magazine*: September 18, 1995, p. 53-56.

Andreas, Steve and Faulkner, Charles, editors. NLP: *The New Technology of Achievement*. New York, N.Y.: William Morrow and Company, Inc., 1994.

Barner, Robert. *Crossing the Minefield*. New York, N.Y.: AMACOM, 1994.

Barnet, Richard J. and Cavanagh, John. *Global Dreams, Imperial Corporations and the New World Order*. New York, N.Y.: Simon & Schuster, 1994.

Bartlett, Christopher A. and Ghoshal, Sumantra. Matrix Management: Not A Structure, A Frame of Mind. *Harvard Business Review*: July-August, 1990, p. 138-142.

Barton, Laurence. *Crisis in Organizations: Managing and Communicating in the Heat of Chaos*. Cincinnati, Oh.: South-Western Publishing Co., 1993.

Baxandall, Rosalyn and Gordon, Linda. *America's Working Women: A Documentary History, 1600 to the present*. New York, N.Y.: W. W. Norton & Company, 1995.

Bernstein, Albert J. and Rozen, Sydney Craft. *Sacred Bull: The Inner Obstacles That Hold You Back At Work and How to Overcome Them*. New York, N.Y.: John Wiley & Sons, Inc., 1994.

Blum, Laurie. *Free Money For Small Businesses and Entrepreneurs*. New York, N.Y.: John Wiley & Sons, Inc., 1995.

Brown, Carolyn M. All Talk, No Action. *Black Enterprise*: Sept., 1995, p. 60-64.

Brown, Thomas. Defining a 'New Social Contract.' *Industry Week*: Aug. 15, 1994, p. 52.

Bruchey, Stuart. *Enterprise: The Dynamic Economy of a Free People*. Cambridge, Ma.: Harvard University Press, 1990.

Caminiti, Susan. What Team Leaders Need to Know. *Fortune Magazine*: February 20, 1995, p. 93-100.

Case, John. A Company of Business People. *INC.*: April, 1993, 79-93.

Chancellor, John. *Peril and Promise: A commentary on America*. New York, N.Y.: Harper & Row Publishers, 1990.

Clark, Scott A. *Unleashing the Hidden Power of Your Growing Business*. New York, N.Y.: AMACOM, 1993.

Connors, Roger and Smith, Tom And Hickman, Craig. *The Oz Principle: Getting Results through Individual and Organizational Accountability*. Englewood Cliffs, N.J.: PTR Prentice Hall, 1994.

Cox, Taylor H. and Blake, Stacy. Managing Cultural Diversity: Implications for Organizational Competitiveness. *Academy of Management Executive*, 1991, Vol. 5, No. 3, p. 45-56.

Delavigne, Kenneth T. and Robertson, J. Daniel. *Deming's Profound Changes: When Will the Sleeping Giant Awaken?* Englewood Cliffs, N.J.: PTR Prentice Hall, 1994.

Driscoll, Dawn-Marie and Goldberg, Carol. *Members of the Club: The Coming of Age of Executive Women*. New York, N.Y.: The Free Press, 1993.

Edmond, Alfred, Jr. The BE 100's: Evolution/Revolution. *Black Enterprise*: June, 1995, p. 85-96.

The Entrepreneur Magazine Small Business Advisor: The One-Stop Information Source for Starting, Managing and Growing a Small Business. New York, N.Y.: John Wiley & Sons, Inc., 1995.

Farnham, Alan. Why the Fortune 50 Club Gets No Respect From Conspiracy Buffs. *Fortune Magazine*: May 15, 1995, p. 210-212.

Fazzi, Robert A. *Management Plus: Maximizing Productivity through Motivation, Performance, and Commitment*. Burr Ridge, Il.: Irwin Professional Publishing, 1994.

Filipczak, Bob. You're On Your Own. *Training*: Jan., 1995, p. 29-36.

Friedman, Milton. *Captialism and Freedom*. Chicago, Il.: The University of Chicago Press, 1982.

Gray, John. *Men Are From Mars, Women Are From Venus: A Practical Guide for Improving Communication and Getting What You Want in Your Relationships.* New York, N.Y.: HarperCollins Publishers, 1992.

Hammer, Michael. *The Reengineering Revolution, A Handbook.* New York, N.Y.: HarperCollins Publishers, 1995.

Harari, Oren. Open the Doors, Tell the Truth. *Management Review*: Jan., 1995, p. 33-35.

Harari, Oren. The Missing Link In Performance. *Management Review*: March, 1995, p. 21-24.

Harari, Oren. The New Job Security: You! *Management Review*: Sept., 1995, p. 29-31.

Hart, Christopher W. L. *Extraordinary Guarantees: A New Way to Build Quality Throughout Your Company & Ensure Satisfaction for Your Customers.* New York, N.Y.: AMACOM, 1993.

Hay, Louise L. *Heal Your Body.* Carson, Ca.: Hay House, Inc., 1994.

Hayes, Cassandra. The New Spin On Corporate Work Teams. *Black Enterprise*: June, 1995, p. 229-234.

Heilbroner, Robert. *Visions of the Future: The Distant Past, Yesterday, Today, and Tomorrow.* New York, N.Y.: Oxford University Press, 1995.

Helgesen, Sally. *The Female Advantage: Women's Ways of Leadership.* New York, N.Y.: Doubleday, 1990

Hequet, Marc. Flat and Happy? *Training*: April, 1995. P. 29-34.

Hoffman, Robert. Ten Reasons You Should Be Using 360-Degree Feedback. *HR Magazine*, April 1995, p. 82-85.

Imparato, Nicholas and Harari, Oren. When New Worlds Stir. *Management Review*, October, 1994, p. 22-28.

Imparato, Nicholas and Harari, Oren. *Jumping the Curve: Innovation and Strategic Choice in an Age of Transition.* San Francisco, Ca.: Jossey-Bass Publishers, 1994.

Jacob, Rahul. The Struggle To Create An Organization For the 21st Century. *Fortune Magazine*: April 3, 1995, p. 90-99.

Jaffe, Denis T. and Scott, Cynthia D. and Tobe, Glenn R. *Rekindling Commitment: How to Revitalize Yourself, Your Work, and Your Organization.* San Francisco, Ca. Jossey-Bass Publishers, 1994.

Jandt, Fred E. *Straight Answers to People Problems.* Burr Ridge, Ill: Irwin Professional Publishing, 1994.

Kennedy, Paul. *Preparing for the Twenty-First Century.* New York, N.Y.: Random House, 1993.

Koonce, Richard. Career Power!: *12 Winning Habits To Get You From Where You Are To Where You Want To Be.* New York, N.Y.: AMACOM, 1994.

Kushel, Gerald. *Reaching The Peak Performance Zone: How to Motivate Yourself and Others to Excel.* New York, N.Y.: AMACOM, 1994.

Labich, Kenneth. Kissing Off. *Fortune Magazine*: February 20, 1995, p. 44-51.

Levering, Robert and Moskowitz, Milton. *The 100 Best Companies to Work for in America.* New York, N.Y.: Penguin Books USA Inc., 1994.

Light, Paul C. *Baby Boomers.* New York, N.Y.: W. W. Norton & Company, 1988.

Mack, Gracian. The Soft Walk Yields the Big Bucks: The Best Investment Partnerships Are the Ones You Don't Hear About. *Black Enterprise*: June, 1995, p. 236-244.

Maddox, Robert C. *Cross-Cultural Problems in International Business: The Role of the Cultural Integration Function.* Westport, Ct.: Quorum Books, 1993.

Marshall, Edward M. *Transforming the Way We Work: The Power of the Collaborative Workplace.* New York, N.Y.: AMACOM, 1995.

Marshall, Ray & Tucker, Marc. *Thinking for a Living: Education and the Wealth of Nations.* New York, N.Y.: HarperCollins Publishers, 1992.

McCoy, Frank. Shattering Glass Ceilings. *Black Enterprise*: Sept., 1985, p. 22.

McKesson, Mike. GM President to Take Wheel as Chairman. *Gannett Suburban Newspapers*: December 5, 1995, p. 5B.

Miller, Paul C. *Big League Business Thinking: The Heavy Hitter's Guide to Top Managerial Performance*. Englewood Cliffs, N.J.: Prentice Hall, 1994.

Morin, William J. *Silent Sabotage: Rescuing Our Careers, Our Companies and Our Lives From the Creeping Paralysis of Anger and Bitterness*. New York, N.Y.: AMACOM, 1995.

Morris, Betsy. Executive Women Confront Midlife Crisis. *Fortune Magazine*, September 18, 1995, p. 60-86

Moss-Kanter, Rosabeth. *The Change Masters*. New York, N.Y.: Simon & Schuster, 1993.

Muhammad, Tariq K. Joint Ventures for Business Opportunities. *Black Enterprise*: June, 1995, p. 220-226.

National Small Business United (NSBU): 1155 15th Street, N.W., Suite 710; Washington, D.C. 20005; 202-293-8830. *Issue Briefs*. April 7, 1995.

National Small Business United. *Issue Briefs. For Delegates To the 1995 White House Conference On Small Business*, June 11-15, 1995.

National Small Business United and Arthur Andersen Enterprise Group. *Survey of Small and Mid-Sized Businesses: Trends for 1995*.

Newman, William H., Editor. *Manager for the Year 2000*. Englewood, N.J.: Prentice Hall, Inc., 1978.

Osbaldeston, Michael. Polling Manager's Opinions on Modified Career Paths. *People Management*: Aug. 10, 1995, p. 47.

Pare, Eileen P. Today's Hot Concept, Tomorrow's Forest Fire. *Fortune Magazine*: May 15, 1995, p. 197-198.

Pension Benefit Guaranty Corporation and Hay/Huggins Company, Inc., *Pension Plan Cost Study*, September, 1990.

Ramirez, Anthony. AT&T Offer: One Said No, One Said Yes: Buyout Decisions By 2 of the 72,000. *The New York Times*: Dec. 10, 1995, p. 3.1, 3.11.

Raskas, Daphne F. and Hanbrick, Donald C. *Multifunctional Managerial Development: A Framework for Evaluating the Options. Organizational Dynamics.* American Management Association, 1992, Reprint.

Reich, Robert B. *Tales of a New America.* New York, N.Y.: Times Books, 1987.

Richman, Tom. What Does Business Really Want From Government. *INC.* May 16, 1996, p. 92-103.

Ritti, R. Richard. *The Ropes to Skip and the Ropes to Know: Studies in Organizational Behavior.* New York, N.Y.: John Wiley & Sons, Inc., 1994.

Sabir, Nadirah Z. Moving On Up. *Black Enterprise.* Sept., 1995, p. 26.

Schine, Eric. Benefits are Being Pecked to Death. *Business Week:* Dec. 4, 1995, p. 42.

Sellers, Patricia. Now Bounce Back! *Fortune Magazine:* May 1, 1995, p. 49-66.

Sellers, Patricia. To Avoid A Trampling, Get Ahead of the Mass. *Fortune Magazine:* May 15, 1995, p. 201-202.

Selz, Michael. Costs of Complying With Federal Rules Weigh More Heavily on Small Firms. *Wall Street Journal:* October 1, 1995, p. FIND PAGE

Selz, Michael. Study Scrutinizes People Who Would Be Entrepreneurs. *The Wall Street Journal:* Dec. 14, 1995, p. B2.

Silbiger, Steven. *The Ten-Day MBA.* New York, N.Y.: William Morrow and Company, Inc., 1993.

Siwolop, Sana. For Small Businesses, Beacons in Cyberspace. *The New York Times:* Dec. 10, 1995, p. B10.

Smith, Timothy K. 40 Years of Winning Ideas with Staying Power. *Fortune Magazine:* May 15, 1995, p. 191.

Steward, Thomas A. A New 500 for the New Economy. *Fortune Magazine:* May 15, 1995, p 166-178.

Steward, Thomas A. Planning A Career in a World Without Managers. *Fortune Magazine:* March 20, 1995, p. 72-78.

Stewart, Thomas A. Which Side Are You On? The Never-Ending War For A Manager's Soul. *Fortune Magazine*: May 15, 1995, p. 12, 124.

Tannen, Deborah. *Talking From 9 To 5: How Women's and Men's Conversational Styles Affect Who Gets Heard, Who Gets Credit, and What Gets Done At Work.* New York, N.Y.: William Morrow and Company, Inc., 1994.

Teller, Laura and Schatz, Warren R. *Small Business, Big Savings: Where and How to Save Money on Everything Your Business Needs.* New York, N.Y.: HarperCollins Publishers, 1995.

The Software Revolution. *Business Week*. Dec. 4, 1995, p. 78-90.

Thomas, R. Roosevelt, Jr. From Affirmative Action to Affirming Diversity. *Harvard Business Review*: March-April, 1990, p. 107-117.

Thompson, John A. with Henningsen, Catherine A. *The Portable Executive.* New York, N.Y.: Simon & Schuster, 1995.

Tomasko, Robert M. *Rethinking the Corporation: The Architecture of Change.* New York, N.Y.: AMACOM, 1993.

U.S. Chamber of Commerce Research Center, *Employee Benefits: 1994 Edition, Survey Data from Benefit Year 1993.*, U.S. Chamber of Commerce, 1994.

U.S. News & World Report. Predictions: Slower Economic Growth Will Leave Many Behind. Dec. 25, 1995, p. 81.

Van Eron, Ann M., Ways To Assess Diversity Success. *HR Magazine*, Aug., 1995, P. 51-52.

Wysocki, Bernard, Jr. High-Tech Jobs Elude New York Region. *The Wall Street Journal*: November 27, 1995, p. A2, A6.

Index

—X—

—Y—

—Z—